"If you remember the COVID-19 pandemic as a suspension of the rules of ordinary life, this compelling book will wake you up. Our confinement indoors was not a refuge from the specters of capital afoot outside. Instead, it allowed our homes to be a proving ground for new capitalist forms that were busy transforming the gendered character of work, shelter, and finance, while turbo-charged currents of debt swirled all around us. *The Home as Laboratory* offers a breathtaking analysis!"
—**Andrew Ross**, author of *Creditocracy and the Case for Debt Refusal*

"Debt, violence, domestic labor, rent, eviction, fintech, production of value, insecurity, poverty, desperation, love, racism, gender mandates and property titles—what happens when we analyze the circuits of financial capital from the place we call home? This brilliant book by leading scholar-activists Luci Cavallero, Verónica Gago, and Liz Mason-Deese is the *Grundrisse* for just such a radical left feminist project. Read it now!
—**Wendy Brown**, author of *In the Ruins of Neoliberalism: The Rise of Anti-Democratic Politics in the West*

"By weaving together detailed social inquiry with innovative theoretical investigations, Luci Cavallero, Verónica Gago, and Liz Mason-Deese provide both a model for research and an orientation for future lines of struggle."
—**Michael Hardt**, author of *The Subversive Seventies* and coauthor of *Bolivia Beyond the Impasse*

"Elegantly translated and lucidly argued, *Home as Laboratory* provides a much-needed post-Covid-19 pandemic analysis of the ways that households have become spaces for experimentation for new dynamics of capital. Expanding existing

Global South feminist theory and resistance practice, Luci Cavallero, Verónica Gago, and Liz Mason-Deese forcefully demonstrate how the intensification of social reproduction exploitation and extraction via apparatuses like debt has been brutal. But *Home as Laboratory* offers us more than just critique, it inspires autonomous feminist struggle and hope wherever the tentacles of financial capitalism need be severed."
—**Jason Thomas Wozniak,** assistant professor at West Chester University, codirector of The Latin American Philosophy of Education Society, and organizer with Debt Collective

Praise for Previous Work

" . . . offers 'a methodology for connecting experience and struggle' and a critique of debt grounded in the belief that economic policies and practices must be reshaped from a feminist perspective to address the conditions and needs of marginalised communities."
—**Patricia Sequeira Brás,** *Modern Times Review*

". . . a slender but powerful condemnation of debt as a tool of patriarchal state violence."
—**Kathleen Field,** *Ethnic and Third World Literatures*

THE HOME AS

LABORATORY

Philadelphia, PA
Brooklyn, NY
commonnotions.org

The Home as Laboratory: Finance, Housing, and Feminist Struggle
©Luci Cavallero, Verónica Gago, and Liz Mason-Deese

This work was supported by a "Right to the Discipline" grant from the Antipode Foundation.

ISBN: 978-1-945335-07-5 | eBook ISBN: 978-1-945335-20-4

Library of Congress Number: 2024931992
10 9 8 7 6 5 4 3 2 1

Common Notions   Common Notions
c/o Interference Archive   c/o Making Worlds Bookstore
314 7th St.   210 S. 45th St.
Brooklyn, NY 11215   Philadelphia, PA 19104

www.commonnotions.org
info@commonnotions.org

Discounted bulk quantities of our books are available for organizing, educational, or fundraising purposes. Please contact Common Notions at the address above for more information.

Cover design by Josh MacPhee
Layout design and typesetting by Suba Murugan

THE HOME AS LABORATORY:

FINANCE, HOUSING, AND

FEMINIST STRUGGLE

LUCI CAVALLERO,
VERÓNICA GAGO, AND
LIZ MASON-DEESE

CONTENTS

ACKNOWLEDGMENTS

First, we would like to thank the two collectives that participated in this work: Asamblea Feminista de la Villa 31 and Inquilinos Agrupados. We would also like to extend our thanks to Malav Kanuga and Erika Biddle from Common Notions, for their editorial work enabling this book to join a catalog of which we are honored to be a part. And to the readers to come who we hope will find resonances here for their own political investigations.

1. THE HOME AS LABORATORY

INTRODUCTION

IN APRIL 2020, a month after restrictions were first imposed in response to the pandemic, we wrote that "debt, housing, and work" were the keys to a post-pandemic feminist agenda.[1] At that time, we could not imagine the duration of COVID-19, even less so how difficult it would be to speak about a "post." During the past two years, we have focused our research and activism on those three lines of inquiry: debt, housing, and work. Although collective encounters became more difficult, they persisted, often becoming smaller and more intermittent, and always with painful and complex contradictions. Undoubtedly, those encounters were strategic for analyzing what was happening and sustaining ourselves.

---

1 Verónica Gago and Luci Cavallero, "Deuda, vivienda, trabajo: Una agenda feminista para la pospandemia" *Revista Anfibia*, April 9, 2020, https://www.revistaanfibia.com/deuda-vivienda-trabajo-una-agenda-feminista-la-pospandemia/.

Amid concern over urgent issues, one thread of conversation insisted upon asking: where will we run into one another if the street is the first thing to be "suspended," if spaces of encounter are the first to be closed? How are we going to meet up if moving about the city is now an epic journey? How can we save time to be together if handling the emergency consumes all our time and energy? What does this mean for a feminist movement whose strength lies in occupying the streets, creating spaces of encounter among differences, and producing our own time?

In the heat of those concerns, another set of questions began arising after the early months of the pandemic: how can we understand the spatiality of feminist demands when "homes" are now considered the privileged site for staying safe? How does this redefinition of the domestic affect the dynamic of our demands? What is new about the idea of *essential labor* in relation to this mutation? How did the feminist movement's insistence on the centrality of domestic space impact public policies implemented in the emergency situation?

We were coming from a moment of effervescence of feminist mobilizations, from occupying the city to dismantling its divisions and closed circuits. The March 8 International Feminist Strike drew hundreds of thousands of women, lesbians, travestis, trans, and nonbinary people to the streets in Buenos Aires. There were nearly constant marches, protests, and assemblies as we put forth our own agenda to expand rights while also attempting to put a stop to new neoliberal austerity measures. It felt like feminism was everywhere. We identified one another through our green handkerchiefs for abortion rights, through our new language and grammar.[2]

---

2 For more on this transnational feminist moment, see Verónica Gago, *The Feminist International: How to Change Everything*, trans. Liz Mason-Deese (New York: Verso Books, 2020).

Then suddenly, the streets emptied. The feminist movement launched initiatives—experiments that defied the initial enclosure: we carried out *ruidazos* [noise-making actions] from our homes, virtual assemblies, food aid, and organized campaigns and networks for abortion, WhatsApp groups for special help, etc. The slogan "feminist networks sustain us" demonstrated the capacity to build emergency infrastructure, re-assemble resources, affects, and knowledges, to insist on accompaniment in new circumstances, to create alerts, to train ourselves in a sense of urgency that would not overwhelm us.

Judith Butler wrote that sometimes the revolution happens when nobody wants to go back home. That issue mutated in front of our eyes. What happens when we have to stay indoors in the face of the fear of contagion? What homes do we go back to? What happens when that same home is besieged by debt and violence? And, when home is not guaranteed and the anxiety of eviction lurks? How do we respond when homes are looted by financial capital and, at the same time, spaces of an unceasing continuum of work?

We went from fleeing and dismantling the domestic as confinement, to experiencing an intensified and everchanging domesticity, having to put up with the overburden of hygiene tasks and, in some cases, having to coinhabit with abusers. Therefore, we thought it was fundamental to use the political tools of street action to open the household up for debate and to experiment with dismantling the home using the tools of struggle. This took place in a specific moment: precisely when the quarantine and its (still open) correlatives broadened the scene of social reproduction. In other words, when the infrastructure that sustains collective life, the territories and bodies that it involves, and the precarity that it supports are revealed. That whole framework was exposed as if with an X-ray.

This work summarizes and condenses the questions that emerged in our political practice during the pandemic and, at the same time, continues our research on the impacts of public and private debt in the everyday lives of women, lesbians, travestis, and trans persons that we have carried out as the *Grupo de Intervención e Investigación Feminista* [Feminist Intervention and Research Group, or GIIF].

We develop two lines of inquiry that draw from political alliances built in the context of feminist mobilizations and organizations. On the one hand, we conducted a series of interviews and conversations with women from Villa 31 and 31 Bis of the City of Buenos Aires—it is one of the oldest and largest informal settlements in the city, home to some 40,000 people and located near the city's main bus and rail stations and port area, in between wealthy and touristic neighborhoods. These interviews, conducted during April and May 2020, allowed us to quickly detect an increase in debt for informal rent and the acceleration of evictions during the pandemic (despite a presidential decree suspending evictions). This linked up with a cartographic project that we had already initiated, in 2019, to discuss what we, along with the Feminist Assembly of Villa 31 and 31 Bis, had denominated "urbanization through debt," showing how the city's urban development plans were based on forcing residents to take out debt for housing.[3] This work was publicly presented during the March 8 International Feminist Strike, in which several differ-

---

3 That cartographic work, produced in collaboration with the Argentinian collective Iconoclasistas (Julia Riser and Pablo Ares), can be found here: https://iconoclasistas.net/portfolio-item/villa-31-31bis/.

ent groups deployed the slogan "Not One Woman Less Without Housing."[4]

On the other hand, as a second line, we built a political alliance with the renters' organization *Inquilinos Agrupados* to create a space of dialogue and exchange between the feminist movement and the tenants' movement, above all, to jointly address issues of household debt and rental housing. These two dimensions connected in a dramatic way during the pandemic, revealing the connections between sexist violence and abuse by property owners, especially against women, lesbians, travestis, and trans people, which we characterized as "property violence."[5]

We have identified the issue of housing, in particular the way household debt reconfigures it, as a key area for feminist investigation. That is also where the dynamics of paid and unpaid labor are reorganized under new coordinates. It is in the household where a series of problems are concentrated that enable us to continue deepening our *feminist reading of debt* and ask: *how has the household become a laboratory?* How does this affect the demands and policies that can be articulated and called for?

In our situated research we see that spatiality of social reproduction is altered and reorganized based on what we

---

4 This is but one example of how slogans demonstrate a collective political intelligence and how the feminist movement has allowed for tracing the connections between multiple types of violence: the call for "not one woman less" proliferates and expands, connecting gender-based violence to—in this case—the violence of oppressive and exclusionary housing policies and of private property in general.

5 Luci Cavallero and Verónica Gago, "A Feminist Perspective on the Battle over Property," trans. Liz Mason-Deese, *Feminist Review*, July 21, 2020, https://femrev.wordpress.com/2020/07/21/a-feminist-perspective-on-the-battle-over-property/.

have detected as four interlinked dynamics that took root in households during the pandemic:

- The increase in household debt for basic goods, as a consequence of income loss and also the emergence of *new* debts (for public services and emergencies);
- The increase in debt for housing (either rental debts or taking out debt to not have to rent) and a greater vulnerability to eviction due to the accumulation of debt. This is combined with the intensification of real estate speculation (on the informal and formal market) through the increase (dollarization) of rents and the restriction of supply;
- The reorganization and intensification of reproductive (especially unpaid) and productive working days in the same space;
- The *intrusion* of financial technology (fintech) in households—through mobile payments, digital wallets, and digital banks.

We are interested in highlighting, analyzing, and connecting these four dynamics because they allow us to understand the household not as a site of isolation, but as a fundamental battle ground. That is, both in the sense of the intrusion of new financial technologies—and therefore, forms of value extraction—and of the reorganization of working days. Political disputes that impact the redefinition of public policies also accumulate in the household. The household, we argue, is a space that brings together novel forms of finance (making the pandemic a financial laboratory) and the intensification of (paid and unpaid) labor. Thus, decisive forms of contemporary valorization are knotted together there, in that space that capital historically sought to portray as an "unproductive" space.

Finance's invasion over the terrain of social reproduction, which is especially targeted at feminized economies, responds to the feminist dispute for the recognition of historically devalued, badly paid, and invisiblized tasks and a desire for economic autonomy. Debt functions as the most important mechanism of wealth accumulation for contemporary capitalism, and simultaneously, as a form of social control. In other words, financialization is not a process that unfolds on its own, but rather it responds, reads, and captures a desire for autonomy expressed by struggles. Thus, mass household indebtedness in recent years is a response to a feminist political protagonism in diverse labor, union, and territorial spheres. It is a type of moralization that seeks to limit and contain the challenge to gender mandates in social reproduction and make the family responsible for assuming the costs of the crisis.

In other words, through these interconnected dynamics, we recognize the household as a battleground over forms of labor and financial extractivism, as well as forms of social control, consolidating a conservative backlash to the threat of feminism.

DEBT IN THE CENTER

In *A FEMINIST Reading of Debt*, we showed how public indebtedness, which accelerated exponentially with the enormous IMF loan taken out by Mauricio Macri's government in 2018, is translated into austerity measures that spill over into homes as household debt.[6] That record-breaking $57 billion loan came, of course, with conditions, many of

---

6 Luci Cavallero and Verónica Gago, *A Feminist Reading of Debt*, trans. Liz Mason-Deese (London: Pluto Press, 2021).

which directly targeted programs and policies for women, lesbians, travestis, and trans people. With neoliberalism, the only thing that trickles down is debt.

In that research, we confirmed an increase in and a proliferation of forms (e.g., formal and informal, banking and nonbanking) of indebtedness that started to be used as a necessary complement to diminishing incomes. The austerity measures imposed by the record external debt, along with inflation and the consequent loss in purchasing power of welfare benefits, pensions, and wages, made taking out debt a requirement for accessing basic goods such as food and medicine.

That reality particularly affected low-income women. One clear example of that phenomenon is the appearance of massive indebtedness through the universal child allowance. Implemented in 2009, as a response to the demands of the unemployed workers' movements, the universal child allowance provides a minimum guaranteed income for heads of household with children. However, like other benefits, the value of the universal child allowance has not kept up with inflation and its purchasing power has severely decreased. For example, a study by the CTA-Autónoma's Social Rights Observatory shows the value of the universal child allowance has depreciated to the point of becoming a mere guarantee for taking out debt.[7] In other words, rather than covering the costs of social reproduction, proof of receiving the allowance serves as eligibility for certain types of formal and informal loans, thus accelerating a cycle of debt.

---

7 CTA-Aútonoma Córdoba, "Fuerte deterioro de la Asignación Universal por Hijo y la Jubilación Mínima," February 28, 2019, https://ctaacordoba.org/fuerte-deterioro-de-la-asignacion-univer-sal-por-hijo-y-la-jubilacion-minima/.

This accelerated impoverishment meant a qualitative and extensive leap in already existing debt in many households: debt to guarantee everyday life and to pay services and utilities became *compulsory*. Debt, as a financial technology, is *channelized* as a response to precarization. The unique element of this phenomenon is that debt is no longer associated with the specific consumption of a good or service, but rather becomes a permanent and obligatory way of making up for diminishing incomes.

A whole new equation is produced between income and debt when that income (whether waged or not) no longer guarantees reproduction. This is an important finding of our research: there is a qualitative change in what debt means in households when it is structured as an everyday mandate, under the formula "take out debt in order to live." That is articulated with a quantitative modification, as its expansion reaches a greater quantity of households and produces a picture of "over-indebtedness," which has recently been recognized as having a direct affect on human rights.[8]

That is what we have called "the financial colonization of social reproduction," in which finance advances over key areas of social reproduction, such as food, health, housing, and education.[9] This advance has clear implications in terms of mechanisms of sexist violence, forcing increasingly dangerous living and working conditions. We developed this analysis by investigating the effects of over-indebtedness in everyday life, focusing on those who maintain household

---

8 J. P. Bohoslavsky, "Deuda privada y derechos Humanos," *Revista Derechos en Acción* 5, no. 15 (Fall 2020).

9 Silvia Federici, Verónica Gago, and Luci Cavallero, "¿Quién le debe a quién? Manifiesto por la desobediencia financiera," in *¿Quién le debe a quién? Ensayos transnacionales de desobediencia financiera* (Buenos Aires: Tinta Limón, 2021), 9–18.

economies in moments of crisis, *putting their bodies on the line in the face of debt.*

Going into debt in order to live, then, has subjective impacts that reorganize everyday life and domesticity and intensify the gender mandates associated with debt repayment. The permanent presence of indebtedness puts debt in the center of life, forcing you to direct all of your energies and efforts to avoiding falling behind on payments, even resorting to taking out loans and aid from family and friends, which can also put intimate and neighborhood relationships at risk. Thinking about that displacement that constructs the centrality of household debt, also implies understanding the forces debt manages to *command* as an organizer of the heterogeneity of increasingly precarious work, including that tied to illegal economies.

An essential dimension in relation to the study of household indebtedness is understanding its relation with, primarily feminized, unpaid work. It is our *feminist perspective on debt* that adds this methodological key—the focus on feminized labor—that was fundamental for understanding the pandemic's impact on domestic spatiality. It is also important to underscore and qualify the relation between debt and labor, because it demonstrates that debt cannot be delinked from its dependence on labor. In opposition to financial abstraction that claims to be a mathematical number or market index, debt *lands* on specific bodies and territories from which it extracts value, which it exploits in a differential way.

We can identify specific forms of labor in the home that underlie the expansion of financial extractivism into the household. And we can map how the necessarily invisibilized and undervalued character of that labor is key to fueling finance.

The need to take out debt in order to live becomes even stronger in single-parent homes, in which women are responsible for children.[10] Thus debt becomes another way of intensifying gender inequalities and, particularly, exploiting unpaid labor. The channelization of household debt *prior to the pandemic* shows that, in this exceptional period, many households had pre-existing debts to which new ones would be added.

We must also elaborate on the conjunctural situation. In Argentina, the pandemic occurred amidst the renegotiation of the country's external debt with the International Monetary Fund (IMF) and private creditors. Public debt functioned as a corset for emergency policies, limited by creditors' demands to keep fiscal debt under control. Thus, the social and health crisis combined with the economic crisis inherited from the previous hyper-neoliberal government (2015–2019), which manifested in a poverty level that amounts to more than 40 percent of the population.[11]

Along with ongoing conditions of precarization, women, lesbians, travestis, and trans and nonbinary people have faced greater difficulty in participating in the labor market due to increased care work in households and neighborhoods. In fact, in the worst moment of the pandemic, there was a 14 percent decrease in economic activity

---

10 An investigation carried out by the Gender and Economy Director of the Ministry of Economy and UNICEF showed that in the first semester of 2020, poverty in single-parent households reached 68.3 percent. See UNICEF Argentina, "Desafíos de las políticas públicas frente a la crisis de los cuidados. El impacto de la pandemia en los hogares con niñas, niños y adolescentes a cargo de mujeres," May 2021, www.unicef.org/argentina/publicaciones-y-datos/desafios-politicas-cuidados-hogares-a-cargo-de-mujeres.

11 Instituto Nacional de Estadística y Censos, "Incidencia de la pobreza y la indigencia en 31 aglomerados urbanos" (Buenos Aires: Ministerio de Economía Argentina, 2020), https://www.indec.gob.ar/uploads/informesdeprensa/eph_pobreza_02_2082FA92E916.pdf.

for female heads of household with children or adolescents, almost four points higher than the general decrease in activity during the same period. These situations functioned as the motor for the appearance of new debts associated with managing everyday life in the harshest moment of the quarantine measures.[12] Suddenly tasks that the state had previously been at least partially responsible for, such as schooling, were left up to individual families (and mostly women within those families) in their homes, who also bore the associated costs such as Internet connections and mobile devices. In other words, the greater the unpaid labor, the greater the debt.

THE DOMESTIC IN DISPUTE

THE POLITICIZATION OF domestic space has long been a banner issue for feminists. Diverse theorizations and practices have made it clear that value is produced there, that the care work that sustains life has historically been made as invisible as necessary, that enclosure within four walls is a political order issued by patriarchal hierarchies.

The feminist movement has long insisted that labor goes beyond those who receive a wage. Thus, the common condition shared among workers is the experience of diverse situations of exploitation and oppression, both beyond and closer to home, rather than the remunerative measure or the privileged terrain of the factory. It also points to the necessary subordination and exploitation of this mass of labor for the existence of waged, recognized, and unionized

---

12 On March 20, 2020, the Argentine federal government implemented the ASPO (Preventative and Obligatory Social Isolation) measures, forcing all but the so-declared "essential workers" to quarantine within their homes or face fines.

labor. However, it is not a matter of choosing one perspective over another, but of *tracing the circuits*.

Maria Mies' concept of "housewifization" is key for the historical grammatical constellation of the domestic.[13] Her question could be put as follows: why does capitalism need to create a space of seclusion and consumption so that women, under the private idea of love, construct a household? When does it occur? How is it related to other historical events? That process of housewifization, Mies says, makes it possible to convert the domestic space into an "internal colony" of the European man while he colonizes "external" territories. Colonization and housewifization are processes that go together and that allow us to analyze their mutually implicated logic: the imbricated structure of colonial and patriarchal capitalism.

The family space, in turn, guarantees a sphere for the creation of necessities, a hygienist euphoria, and the subsumption of reproduction to heteronormative family logics. Mies states, "housewifization means the externalization, or ex-territorialization of costs which otherwise would have to be covered by the capitalists. This means women's labour is considered a natural resource, freely available like air and water."[14]

Thus, an army of "hidden workers" is produced. Male proletarianization is impossible without the housewifization of women, there can be no external colonization without internal colonization. Housewifization is also assembled with processes of proletarianization, especially in peripheral countries: a woman works in a workshop or factory or hospital and is an "invisible worker" at the same

---

13 Maria Mies, *Patriarchy and Accumulation on a World Scale: Women in the International Division of Labour* (London: Zed Books, 1998).

14 Mies, *Patriarchy and Accumulation*, 110.

time. "Exclusively" being a housewife is a figure that has never been universal, as Black, Indigenous, and decolonial feminists have clearly shown.[15]

Today we are called upon to rethink the dynamics of contemporary housewifization, precisely when the domestic space is being rapidly and dramatically reconfigured. This requires, above all, recognizing the reality of countries such as Argentina, in which housewifization and colonization overlap and intersect. It is the peripheral regions of the world-economy where the domestic has other borders and folds that expand to the neighborhood and the community, from which its confinement is contested.

It is fundamental to understand the domestic as the production of a space of obligatory and free labor. Silvia Federici systematized this in her now classic *Caliban and the Witch*.[16] The domestic is produced in capitalism as a space of "enclosure": women are *confined* to the household, they are limited to that sphere baptized as "private," they are stripped of their capacity of labor and political leadership. What we take from Federici, whose theorization was nourished by the political experience of the Wages for Housework campaign in the 1970s, is the specific mode of exploitation that capitalism organizes for certain "domesticated" bodies, which first requires that the work lose social prestige and that its web of cooperation be isolated.[17] Only in that way can its enclosure and privatization, its natural-

---

15 See, for example, Angela Davis, *Women, Race, and Class* (New York: Vintage Books, 1983).

16 Silvia Federici, *Caliban and the Witch: Women, the Body, and Primitive Accumulation* (Brooklyn: Autonomedia, 2004).

17 Silvia Federici and Arlen Austin, eds., *Wages for Housework. The New York Committee 1972–1977: History, Theory, Documents* (Brooklyn: Autonomedia, 2017).

ization as "raw material" to be exploited without a wage, be justified.

Later, that work would be connected with strict gender mandates (regarding who should do care work, raise children, cook, etc.) that seek to romanticize it as if it were a solely affective task, detached from its exhausting and hierarchical organization. In turn, the forms of work inaugurated under colonial slavery persist with the new articulations of labor under strict hierarchies of race, class, and gender.

The so-called new waves of primitive accumulation studied by Rosa Luxemburg are how forms of violence are updated when it comes to exploiting the labor force through its sexual and international division. This allows for subordinating the relation between genders (and, more generally, toward feminized bodies) and having access to free labor, while that labor is politically devalued.[18] During the last four decades of capital's neoliberal stage, those mechanisms of primitive accumulation have been relaunched and intensified. Forms of dispossession of natural resources and common goods, the privatization of public services, the increase in unremunerated labor, and the financialization of social reproduction have come to the forefront.

ESSENTIALNESS AND REMUNERATION: SEPARATE ISSUES

HYPOTHESIZING THAT THE household functions as a laboratory during the pandemic directly led us to questions that

---

18 See David Harvey, *The New Imperialism* (Oxford: Oxford University Press, 2003) and Rosa Luxemburg, *The Accumulation of Capital*, trans. A Schwarzschild (New York: Monthly Review Press, 1968).

had been raised by feminist mobilizations in previous years: how is a workday without a fixed duration counted? What is "produced" in the home? How is its value calculated? Who should pay for that work? Who carries out the tasks of reproduction? How does that work overflow beyond the walls of the home?

Recognizing that domestic labor must be unpaid as a condition of possibility for capitalist profit displaces the question about value production: it is not a matter of whether or not value is produced (given that of course it is), but rather why it is necessary to deny that and force that labor to go unpaid. Ultimately, it is a matter of identifying the political apparatus that guarantees those conditions each time and, later, the strategies for its recognition, remuneration, and, above all, its reorganization.

Here it is important to remember that there is a whole debate over how to reread the "measure of value" and the crisis of the value form associated with the wage that allows for discussing what happens with domestic labor. Feminist theorizations with different analyses have incorporated notions such as affect-value or community-value to think about other forms of value and measure other productive instances that exceed the mediation of the wage.[19]

The difficulty of that "measurement" in certain spheres and tasks is not a sign that value is not being produced. We could synthesize that a feminist perspective destabilizes calculation and measure according to capital's rationality. "Unmeasurability," which takes into account invisibilized and uncounted forms of work and even the subjective history of oppressions, describes reproductive work, as well as work in the peripheries. That unmeasurability, as a source of excess, also expresses the (indeterminate) power (*poten-*

---

19 Cristina Morini, *Por amor o a la fuerza* (Madrid: Traficantes de Sueños, 2014).

cia) of labor as living labor. In other words, the problems to which reproductive labor leads us allow us to analyze general dynamics of labor associated with the patriarchal-colonial dynamic of segmented precarization of the labor force.

However, that unmeasurability is also taken advantage of by financial apparatuses that pounce on different forms of collective wealth through different modes of *capture*. Finance takes root in households because that is the space in which a "microscopic pedagogy" is practiced that produces habits.[20] According to Toni Negri, there are two elements that must be taken into account in households, where "attitudes that become forms and architectural elements that become machines" are elaborated.[21] Forms and machines, he adds, are, from a subjective point of view, "the digitalization of society and the computerization of the city." Both elements "make it possible to work at home in a situation in which the architectural elements and communication networks are inserted in housing itself."

If the "debt economy" is expressed, in Maurizio Lazzarato and Éric Alliez's words, through different forms of war, we are particularly interested in thinking about how it attacks social reproduction and establishes its battlefield there.[22] At the same time, it does so in the manner of a dispute over the subjectivities that act on the same plane of the microscopic and reiterative formation of our habits for managing everyday life in the midst of precarity.

---

20 Lion Murard and Patrick Zylberman, *Le petit travailleur infatigable ou le prolétaire régénéré (Villes-usines, habitat et intimités au XIXè siècle)* (Paris: Recherches, 1976).

21 Antonio Negri, *De la fábrica a la metrópolis* (Buenos Aires: Cactus, 2020).

22 Éric Alliez and Maurizio Lazzarato, *Wars and Capital*, trans. Ames Hodges (Los Angeles: Semiotext(e), 2018).

In recent years, through massive feminist mobilizations, occupying the streets has played an important role in "deconfining" households, critiquing their borders, and confronting the invisibilization and privatization of the tasks carried out within them. Feminism has shifted the lens of productive spatialities and, as Federici argues, allows for counting the full duration of the working day, including what takes place in kitchens and bedrooms.[23] We could also add neighborhoods and community spaces. It is in that fabric of laborious spatiality where the work of reproducing life takes place and in which work is carried out that mixes self-management with scarce public resources, carrying out social tasks that complete and/or replace deficient or nonexistent services, at the same time as they sustain a labor force subjected to ever more precarity.

New uses and locations emerge: houses that become day cares in the face of their lack of availability in certain neighborhoods; soup kitchens that are also extended to homes because there is not enough room; markets that host an open-air doctor's office; streets and school spaces fixed by neighborhood groups; the overburdening of community networks responding to gender- based violence.

It is this world of work generally associated with images of the "submerged" and the hidden (as is the *domestic* itself), that makes it possible for social organization to shape everyday life even in the midst of a crisis such as the current one. These multifaceted and multisector labor dynamics are primarily led by women, lesbians, travestis, and trans people. They are the ones who deploy an enormous amount of free, barely subsidized, "nonregistered," precaritized labor. They work in neighborhood health clinics, community soup kitchens or gardens, pick up recycling, and organize street

---

23 Silvia Federici, *Patriarchy of the Wage: Notes on Marx, Gender, and Feminism* (PM Press: 2021).

cleaning. They provide support networks and safe houses in instances of intra-household violence. Some of this work is recognized and paid for by the state or community organizations, but, for the most part, it goes unrecognized and unpaid.

With the crisis accelerated by the pandemic, even the borders of precarization have become more diffuse. This was shown by the "appearance" of eleven million people who requested the "Emergency Family Income" (IFE). The government of Alberto Fernández implemented two main programs in 2020 in response to the crisis: IFE, aid offered to low-income families to make up for the decrease in wages during the pandemic and quarantine measures; and the Emergency Assistance for Labor and Production Program (ATP). Additional temporary programs included freezing mortgage payments, zero interest loans for the self-employed, and a one-year decree prohibiting housing evictions. The IFE was the most significant aid. The state calculated that it would receive requests from three million people, but the demand came from a quarter of the country's population. The program lasted eight months and reached 8.9 million people. The program itself was part of what we refer to as "bankarization," since the payments could only be obtained through bank accounts and digital technology: two million people opened a bank account for the first time to be able to receive the payment. This new subsidy, in addition to already existing ones, revealed forms of precarity that are generally not registered as "poverty" by the standard indexes and that, nonetheless, mark a profound restructuring of the everyday capacity to generate income. The IFE was discontinued in December 2020, in the context of negotiations with the International Monetary Fund (IMF).

There was also a dispute over the incorporation of domestic workers into the benefit program, since it was one of the sectors most harmed by restrictions on mobility, as well as historically one of the lowest paid sectors that, at the same time, is a key way for women to enter the labor market. Emergency decrees declared caregiving tasks—providing necessary assistance to the elderly, ill, or young—to be essential, allowing those workers to move about despite quarantine restrictions. However, other domestic workers were expected to follow quarantine protocols and stay at home, while their employers continued paying them. Of course, since domestic work is one of the sectors that is hardest to regulate, precisely because it takes place within the home, in practice this meant that many domestic workers completely lost their incomes. These issues were highlighted, and disputed, by the feminist movement. Thus, the discussion about what sectors, jobs, and tasks should be aided in the midst of the emergency situation did not take place in abstract terms. It was framed by struggles for the recognition and remuneration of informalized, precarious, and feminized work.

Based on uses of the category of *essential work* that were popularized during the pandemic, can we map a paradoxical reclassification of the crisis of waged labor and a tendency toward the intensification of the work least recognized as such? What bodies sustain that essentialness and at what (physical and psychological) costs?

When we speak about the work of reproduction we refer to the work that is carried out in *domestic territories* that not only include homes, but that constitute spaces of collective, territorial, neighborhood reproduction in the face of systematic dispossession that deprived those places of basic forms of livelihood. That work deployed in those domestic territories, which expands the very spatiality of the domestic, is what responds to everyday urgent needs: from the food crisis to the health crisis, including gender-based violence and the housing crisis.

It was precisely that work that condenses the tasks carried out by women, lesbians, travestis, and trans persons, small-scale farmers and peasants, migrants, those historically not recognized as workers and ignored in their productive capacity that took center stage in the pandemic. Unlimited working days, marked by constant availability in the face of the emergency, the invention of resources in the face of scarcity, putting in play knowledges that have been accumulated as a way of confronting everyday dispossession, were called *essential*. That essentialness also created a common ground between different types and spatialities of reproductive work, between state health care and education workers and those who carry out community management and domestic work.

In the field of registered wage work, that which is traditionally defined as productive, the category of essential work enabled a dispute about the criteria of its definition. In Argentina, workers in companies such as those making alcoholic beverages, snack foods, and oil pipes claimed they were *not* essential, in a conflict with their management that did not allow them to suspend their tasks and forced them to continue working.[24] In Chile and Brazil, that same battle was directly related with the governments' delay and reluctance to declare a quarantine. Chile's British American Tobacco Company, in a striking example, claimed to be essential production, despite the high level of contagion among its workers. Which sectors were included in the category of "essential" became a sort of test of companies'

---

24 Victoria Basualdo and Pablo Peláez, "Procesos de conflictividad laboral en el marco de la pandemia del COVID-19 en Argentina (marzo–mayo 2020)," *FLACSO Argentina* (June 2020), https://www.flacso.org.ar/publicaciones/procesos-de-conflictividad-laboral-en-el-marco-de-la-pandemia-del-covid-19-en-argentina-marzo-mayo-2020/.

power to confront the measures that forced them not to fire workers, as a way of obtaining state subsidies to pay wages and, even, to force the grammar of labor-management agreements on pay cuts in a "peaceful framework." Later, in a second moment, registered waged workers who were classified as essential demanded better health and safety conditions in their workplaces, thus organizing the translation of that essentialness into terms of rights and protections. That call was particularly notable in unions of health care workers and grocery store workers.

From a feminist perspective on labor, two important disputes took place in Argentina. First, the demand to consider accompaniment in cases of gender-based violence essential work, which would allow for those carrying out accompaniment to move through the neighborhood and city despite quarantine measures. Eventually, in response to feminist demands, those types of tasks were recognized as essential by the national government. Second, there was a dispute over recognizing the care work carried out in households and neighborhoods, especially by community organizations and social movements, from running soup kitchens and community health clinics to trash collection and other hygiene tasks, as essential. Slogans emerged from that struggle such as "We are on the front lines" or "We are essential" as a coalition of grassroots organizations demanded that the state pay those workers responsible for containing the virus in some of the country's poorest neighborhoods.[25]

This twist in recognizing community work under the baptism of essential is complex. To a large extent, it was recognized by codifying it in the key of abnegation, heroism,

25 Laura Vales, "Piden que los trabajadores de comedores cobren un salario," *Página/12* (July 24, 2020), https://www.pagina12.com.ar/280285-piden-que-los-trabajadores-de-comedores-cobren-un-salario.

and gender mandates. Thus, it lies in tension with the work done by the feminist movement, through years of mobilization, debate, and organization, demanding rights and wages for that work, and attributing a political value and territorial leadership to it while also denaturalizing it as women's work.

Essential work thus condenses a strong paradox: it names a re-naturalization of those tasks and their association with certain bodies, which are now applauded for their work, but yet still not sufficiently remunerated. This produces a particular twist: it is spoken of as work but, upon classifying it as *essential*, it seems to cease to be so. Its value is recognized but that value seems to be fundamentally symbolic and emergency-based.

We see this practiced on a large scale on those tasks and many jobs connected to social reproduction: it is the historical maneuver of the naturalization of the work of reproduction, only now it is out in the open and no longer in the enclosure of the household sphere. Meanwhile, *at the same time*, there is a "return" to the home under the mode of expanding telework, reproductive tasks, and new care responsibilities.

While one reading of essential work could be that it seeks to legitimize the gratuity and/or insufficient remuneration of certain tasks carried out in domestic territories, we can also identify the inscription of accumulated struggles there. Would it have been possible to make this explicit connection between the essential and the reproductive if the feminist movement had not already politicized care at the mass level? In other words, even before the pandemic, care, reproductive, and domestic labor were already on the forefront of the political agenda because of the work of the feminist movement.

We are in a moment in which the dispute over forms of labor is fundamental. The tension between essentialness-recognition-remuneration has been on the agenda raised by feminist movements through the calls for international feminist strikes in recent years. The demands are organized in a way that takes seriously how feminism has expanded the concept of labor, shining the spotlight on social reproduction.

Feminist diagnoses of the pauperization of the conditions of waged, domestic, and migrant labor—through accelerated processes of precarization in the pandemic—hold such validity both because they expand the notion of labor (in order to enable the recognition of their essential nature) and because they contemplate union strategies to intervene in that expansion.

Demonstrating the multiplication of working days within the same day, the exhaustion involved in putting one's body on the line in the crisis, simultaneous telework with schooling at home, all the juggling to make ends meet with incomes that decrease at the rate of inflation, the replacement of the state's responsibilities by overburdened networks with insufficient resources—this expands the field of struggles, points to unpaid labor, and disputes recognition and resources that include, while also going beyond, the wage.

It becomes necessary to rethink the spatiality and conflictivity of labor (and the modes of understanding it, measuring it, visibilizing it) to also understand its dynamics of struggle, resistance, and dispute over the commonwealth. This is true even today, when the very notion of essential work appears to have fallen out of style.

THE FACTORY-HOME

IN THE 1970s, the Wages for Housework Campaign deployed the slogan "the home is our factory." Today, the demand for productivity is fused with the household, producing a true "home-factory." It is a productive-repro-ductive spatiality that functions indoors every day of the week with no time limits, reissuing historical forms of work in the home. This is also connected to the becoming factory of the territory, in a broader sense of the domestic as that which we referred to above as "domestic territories."

In Argentina, several pioneering studies have debated definitions of the domestic. Elizabeth Jelin and María del Carmen Feijoó propose "domesticity" is a shifting con-cept—its meaning shifts according to the activities that are associated with that sphere and their sex-gender divisions.[26] Along the same line, Paula Aguilar understands domesticity as "an effect of the whole, of multiple practices and dis-courses, forms of problematization, that converge, in the definition of moral attributes, social spaces, and specific tasks as corresponding to the 'domestic.'" The Argentine sociologist continues to make a highly relevant point, asking if "there is something like a specifically neoliberal mode of making the domestic intelligible, and, thus, gov-ernable in the design of social policies in the context of a new social question."[27]

Today we see that capital seeks to take advantage of the pandemic crisis by over-exploiting domestic space. Is this imperative to work from home, educate children from home, of the home-office, home-school, and so on, taking that demand of productivity of the factory-home to the extreme? And will its temporality outlast the pandemic?

---

26 Elizabeth Jelin and María del Carmen Feijoó, *Trabajo y familia en el ciclo de vida femenino: el caso de los sectores populares de Buenos Aires* (Buenos Aires: CEDES, 1989).

27 Paula Aguilar, *El hogar como problema y como solución: una mi-rada genealógica de la domesticidad a través de las políticas sociales. Argentina 1890–1940* (Buenos Aires: Ediciones del Centro Cul-tural de la Cooperación Floreal Gorini, 2014), 12–15.

Furthermore, we must ask: what type of homes are we talking about? Interiors with little space, saturated with family burdens, that now must be productive with jobs that, until recently, were carried out in offices, factories, workshops, retail spaces, schools, and universities. There is a demand for hyperactivity at the same time as we move increasingly less and mobility is increasingly segmented. Meanwhile, capitalism minimizes its costs: we, the workers, pay the rent and utilities for "our" workplaces, with remote work we do not "need" transportation to go to work, which cheapens our "availability" and makes it more flexible. Quotas and credit are offered to "equip ourselves." Platforms force us to pay "storage" or contract them to work remotely.

At the same time, delivery platforms ensure precarious distribution logistics and supply some of the consumption of those hyperproductive homes, that now almost do not have time to address certain basic needs, such as cooking. It must be recognized that the hyper-precarious delivery work, which along with low wages also suffered increased exposure to COVID, is the flipside that makes working from home an option for so many.

We are proletarianized indoors, as they attempt to suck the air out of the outside. It is no coincidence that, in Argentina, it was precisely during the pandemic that the number of hours involved in care work and domestic work in general started to be counted, demonstrating that it is the "industry" that has grown the most in this period.[28]

If we already talked about a triple working day for women, lesbians, travestis, and trans persons (waged work,

---

28 Ministerio de economía, "Los cuidados, un sector económico estratégico. Medición del aporte del Trabajo Doméstico y de Cuidados no Remunerado al Producto Bruto Interno" (2020), https://www.argentina.gob.ar/sites/default/files/los_cuidados_-_un_sector_economico_estrategico_0.pdf.

domestic work, and community work), today we are faced with the near impossibility of distinguishing between the hours in which each one of those working days occurs. On the one hand, because there is a spatial indistinction in which everything mixes together. On the other hand, because the working day does not only expand in terms of the number of hours, but is also intensified due to the lack of distinctions and taking on ever more tasks. Every moment is a triple working day in itself. While you tele-work, you take care of others; while you do community work, you attend your family's needs; while you work at home, you do the paperwork to receive benefits, while also getting dinner on the table.

During the pandemic, the increase in reproductive work has been brutal: from taking responsibility for children's schooling inside homes to different forms of care work, including greater demands for cleaning and tele-work. That increase in reproductive work, paradoxically, has generated more debt. Unrecognized work in the home is translated into income inequality that, in turn, becomes a mechanism of debt. It is this situation, furthermore, that produces a direct relation with the growth of illegal economies as offers of employment in highly vulnerable situations, and thus, contribute to the increase in violence.

Thus, households themselves have become spaces of experimentation for new dynamics of capital. A sort of continuum of tasks seems to take root there that even defies the division between the public and the private that structures the labor market. Therefore, our hypothesis is that we are facing a restructuring of class relations that takes the sphere of reproduction as its primary stage.

Even after the most extreme moments of the health emergency, those advances in labor flexibilization that atomize workers and make us even more precarious have not stopped. To the contrary, they seem to have been established as the new norm. In fact, data on job recovery at the end of 2021 showed that a major part of this recovery occurred in increasingly precarious jobs.[29]

Drawing on recent research, Ursula Huws describes a graphic "vicious cycle" to connect precarious work for platforms services to homes, in which people work ever more because they need money while they have less time for domestic tasks, which are supplied by those delivery platforms. She writes: "In the desperation to obtain more money, we work increasingly more, but later we run against the limit that we don't have time to cook, maintain our homes, or care for our families. Exhausted, we thus resort to platforms for prepared food and domestic or care services. Thus this unleashes a downward spiral in which the lack of money leads to a lack of time, but the ends never meet and capitalism benefits from one point to the other."[30]

Is this the outsourcing of housewifization? That would be one way to name this process that appears as contradictory, but rather is a matter of the reclassification in which domestic tasks are externalized while productive dynamics that were previously developed outside the domestic space are internalized. It is a political and spatial problem that poses the question of the forms of confrontation of the domestic and its reconfigurations.

Let's go further: we propose analyzing what happens in broader speculative financial circuits *starting from the household*. We analyze how the place of confinement in the home

---

29 IPyPP, "Recomposición del empleo y aumento de la precariedad. Los datos del mercado de trabajo al tercer trimestre 2021" (December 2021), https://ipypp.org.ar/descargas/2021/3er%20 trimestre%202021.pdf.

30 Ursula Huws, "Un círculo vicioso que no se aguanta más," *Jacobin America Latina*, no. 4, *¿Adiós al proletariado?*, August 11, 2021, https://jacobinlat.com/2021/11/08/un-circulo-vicioso-que-no-se-aguanta-mas/.

has become a space of financial valorization and how it has accelerated during the pandemic. In this way we invert the traditional reading: from above to below. Everyday spaces of the home have become financial "terminals" (to which financial apparatuses of debt, the mediation of incomes and consumption, and the capture of rent are directed), but they are also intensified as spaces of the *production* of value (reproductive labor, telework, and new modes of home work) that are exploited by different speculative circuits.

In this sense, we want to understand what we hypothesize as an increasingly exploited and precarious domesticity that has been altered through the long months of the unequal suspension of incomes and perception of rents. In that domesticity, debt paradoxically demonstrates the combination between the possibility of resolving the emergency (taking out debt to pay rent and avoid eviction, for example) and the increase in the extraction of value (capture and command of labor to come), uniquely combining domestic space and financial technology.

THE INDEBTED HOME

DURING THE QUARANTINE, we argued that, in methodological terms, it was necessary to think about the pandemic not as a "generalized suspension," but rather based on the question of which sectors accelerated their own profit logics.[31] Undoubtedly, real estate speculation not only did not stop, but even increased due to the generalized increase in rental prices (both in the formal and informal market) and the

---

31 Luci Cavallero and Verónica Gago, "Contra el extractivismo financiero: extender la cuarentena a las finanzas," Instituto Tricontinental (June 22, 2020), https://thetricontinental.org/es/argentina/fp-cavalleroygago/.

increase in evictions due to the accumulation of debt by renters. This process came together with the financialization of social reproduction that we discussed previously. In this sense, we want to propose that a central aspect of the becoming laboratory of the home, and specifically as a laboratory of the intensification of the extraction of rents, has been the positive feedback loop between two problematics: the increase in household indebtedness along with the increase in the price of rent due to market deregulation.

The model of financial valorization applied to housing is deployed as extractivism over urban territories, energized by real estate capital in alliance with financial capital. The speculative maneuvers of investors thus lead to the financialization of housing, in both the informal and the formal market, connecting housing with global financial circuits.

How does this happen? There are several different processes. First, people go into debt to obtain the title to a housing unit in an urban redevelopment or relocation process. Second, rents increase (and are dollarized) as an affect of real estate speculation over land since the state does not regulate the value of the square meter of housing's sale value. Third, through the conception of housing as a "financial asset," titles are bought and sold through investment funds, in a process that has only recently begun in Argentina but has already become quite common and disastrous in other areas of the world. And, fourth, residents are directly displaced and evicted to turn certain areas into new real estate business.

Next, we will take a deeper look at this phenomenon through our research in Villa 31 and 31 Bis, which demonstrates the dynamics of the informal housing market in the City of Buenos Aires, and, on the other hand, the process of organization deployed by Inquilinos Agrupados that expresses the consolidation of a subject of struggle during the pandemic: tenants.

FEMINIST ASSEMBLY OF VILLA 31 AND 31 BIS

SELF-CONSTRUCTED SPACES, SUCH AS *villas* (shantytowns) and "informal" settlements, have become a land reserve for a new shift of the financial-real estate frontier. These are spaces where it is "easier" to evict and cheaper to produce that expansion. According to Raquel Rolnik, financial power expands through a process of the "colonization of land and housing" that transforms our territories, landscapes, houses, and lives.[32]

We have investigated how this process occurs through the experience of the Feminist Assembly of Villa 31 and 31 Bis's resistance to the urbanization process carried out by the Government of Buenos Aires, which, as the organizations say, is far from being the real urbanization that the movement has historically demanded.

Villa 31 and 31 Bis is one of Buenos Aires' oldest and largest urban settlements with over 40,000 residents. The area in which Villa 31 and 31 Bis is located is strategic because it is in the center of the city, between the wealthy neighborhoods of Recoleta and Puerto Madero, across the tracks from the city's main rail station, and borders port logistics spaces. It is also part of a real estate reorganization of waterfront areas that has sought to redevelop the waterfront area for tourists and investors. It is a prime example of metropolitan management because of the brutal financial conquest of land and housing. In December 2015, the redevelopment of the neighborhood was relaunched thanks to a million-dollar loan from the Inter-American Development

32 Raquel Rolnik, *Urban Warfare: Housing under the Empire of Finance* (New York: Verso Books, 2019).

Bank and a specific secretariat was created for that objective. Since that moment, real estate capital's advance has taken on new impetus. In December 2018, the Legislature of the City of Buenos Aires passed Law No. 6129 which complemented previous Law 3343, which proposes modifications that annul points of the original law designed to promote the definitive settlement of inhabitants of Villa 31 and 31 Bis.

A month after that law was passed, the Feminist Assembly of Villa 31 and 31 Bis was founded, to organize in the neighborhood for the national feminist strike in repudiation of the judicial ruling that absolved those responsible for the feminicide of Lucía Pérez.[33] The Feminist Assembly, an alliance of women's groups from different organizations and collectives, began organizing around issues of gender-based violence in the neighborhood, carrying out mobilizations in response to specific instances or cases, as well as to connect feminist organizing in the neighborhood with the broader feminist movement. It was then that, as part of the Ni Una Menos Collective, we started our political articulation and common political work.

During 2020, along with the assembly, we produced a cartographic map of the housing situation, developing our analysis of what we denominated "urbanization by debt." This project as elaborated as a continuation of assemblies carried out in 2019 that brought together the Feminist Assembly of Villa 31 and 31 Bis and the Ni Una Menos Collective, called "Urbanization in a Feminist Register: Against Indebtedness and Gender Mandates." Those encounters focused on delving into two lines of

---

33 It was the brutal feminicide of Lucía Pérez that motivated the first national women's strike in Argentina, in October 2019. Later, the absolution of her killers would motivate another wave of protests across the country.

work and inquiry: "Precarities and Debt" and "Feminist Territorial Organization."

Following this line of action, in March 2020, in the context of the March 8 International Feminist Strike, the feminist assembly carried out an action at the doors of Banco Santander under the banner, "What they call love is unpaid work. We want to live, free and debt free!" This action called attention to the bank's role as an emblem of a type of urbanization in a register of "social integration" (the banking institution as the civilizational standard) at the same time as it points to integration with financial mediation as both a corporate and government policy.

While the civilian-military dictatorship (1976–1983) failed in its plan to evict the villa through direct violence, now we see that this eviction occurs through other means, through the violence of debt. In *A Feminist Reading of Debt*, we formulated the notion of "urbanization through debt" to render visible the mechanisms of evictions concealed by the debt posed by this urban development project. That project not only attempts to force residents to resettle and take out debt for the new housing in the process, but also forces them into housing built with poor materials that are advertised as models of neighborhood modernization.

HOUSE TITLING BASED ON DEBTS

HOUSING IN THESE recently constructed complexes is granted through credit, after one abandons one's land and home, built with great personal effort. Residents become "virtual" property owners, as the banks retain the property titles as long as the commitment to the monthly debt repayment lasts. Along with the credit payment, residents must pay public services, expenses, and taxes: an accumulation that turns into debt that is impossible to pay off. This debt is used to justify future evictions, made possible by legal means. The contract that promises the property title, even if it is presented as founded between equal parties, is based on the premise that it will not be fulfilled. It is that set of accumulated obligations that become unpayable debts that activate the machinery of "legal" evictions.

Law No. 6129, passed in December 2018 enabled, in point 7 of the deed model, mortgages to be converted into bills. This made it possible for investment groups to buy them, transferring a debt that residents originally had with the state into private hands. The sale of mortgage debt titles to third parties become a concrete mechanism for consummating the financialization of the housing "asset."

The poor quality of the new housing is also worth remarking on. According to reports from residents, awardees in the sector denominated the "Container" (in reference to the container base that the houses simulate, in an analogy with the port area, which points to an interesting connection between real estate speculation over the landscape and logistics), the walls are not soundproof and it is impossible to expand or modify the construction, creating difficulties when family dynamics change and limiting possibilities for commercial enterprises, both key aspects of self-constructed housing. In turn, the entire service installation depends on the electrical connection in a neighborhood with frequent power outages. This mode of cheap and precarious construction is accounted for by both the type of investment and the subtext of nondurable, not fully inhabitable houses, which also seems to encourage residents to sell them.

The feminist assembly has rendered visible and critiqued the family-based criteria by which property deeds are assigned. The assembly, through the organization of women, lesbians, travestis, and trans persons, has shown that the deeds are granted to women or men who live in heterosexual families with children, privileging a cis-hetero-sexist criteria that punishes lives lived outside that norm. In parallel, misnomered "single mothers," female heads of single-parent households—which constitute the majority in the neighborhood—are relegated to the end of the list, adding conflicts due to family breakdowns. There have also been cases in which the property title has been granted to men who have been accused of gender-based violence, which forces women to live in the same home with their aggressors. In that sense, in November 2019, the feminist assembly carried out a mobilization in support of a neighborhood resident who was identified as a "victim of a sexist violence and urban development," denouncing that a housing solution was granted to her reported abuser and not to her. That same month, the first plurinational trans villera LGBTTIQ+ parade was held in Villa 31 and 31 Bis. The LGBTTIQ+ movement actively participates in the Feminist Assembly and has been directly involved in resistance to the urbanization plan.

REINFORCING THE FAMILY AND GENDER MANDATES THROUGH PROPERTY TITLES

CARRYING OUT COMMON actions, mutual listening of stories, and elaboration in the assembly allow for affirming that the official strategy, that brings together business and government interests, is a combination of abuse, threats, untimely demolitions, and tactics to create divisions between families, between renters and property owners, between migrants and Argentinians. Despite the sanction of Law No. 3343 in 2009 for the urban development of Villa 31, the city's governing party (PRO) never approved the project and wants to sell the land to pay the debt taken out to make the Paseo del Bajo highway.

Urbanization through debt thus generates a triple situation of violence: sexist, housing, and institutional violence. The assembly has denounced the fact that housing solutions are scarce, precarious, and lack a feminist perspective. That is the case of the current housing subsidy that requires that women, lesbians, travestis, and trans persons prove that they are living on the street, even with children, to be able to receive it. In that way, the available assistance turns into bureaucratic labyrinths with re-victimizing requirements.

Community networks in the neighborhood are what sustain, intervene, care for, and, in some cases, stop situations of violence from escalating. To the contrary, the action of security forces plays a major role in ensuring impunity for gender-based violence.

The pandemic crisis intensifies the division between property owners and non-owners in a family-based register. How? When rent can no longer be paid due to restricted incomes, inherited or marital housing is reinforced as the only way of ensuring a home. This excludes realities such as those of the LGBTTIQ+ population, which is largely disinherited and has other forms of cohabitation beyond heterosexual conjugality. Thus, when wages and benefits are not enough, family property becomes the available income, demonstrating that it is nearly impossible to exercise that right beyond the jurisdiction of the family. The home, in this way, is once again the site from which to "re-order" what is being challenged. Furthermore, this was already the space in which gender mandates associated with tasks of reproduction were historically fixed, with their long work-days of invisibilized labor. Questioning what we call the "home" is also to problematize the private assumption of responsibility in the crisis.

#STAYATHOME

PREVIOUSLY EXISTING HOUSING problems became more urgent with the pandemic. The imperative to Stay at Home demonstrated the limits and difficulties in a context of an informal real estate market subjected to intense speculation, houses without basic services, and evictions and threats. All of this combined with an increase in gender-based violence in the confinement and economic crisis. Therefore, it is essential to render visible the domestic space as a nucleus of the reproduction of life, subjected to new dynamics of exploitation and overburden of work.

Cleaning and safety protocols for the neighborhood remained in the hands of social and feminist organizations, which were placed on the front lines of the emergency situation. Especially in working class neighborhoods and slums, the state abdicated its responsibilities and community organizations took on basic responsibilities of sanitation, health care, education, and food provision. Care for one's self and the community became difficult because of systematic water outages, which made it impossible to follow the hygiene and social distancing recommendations.[34]

The pandemic, and associated quarantine measures, led to a severe reduction in incomes, especially for work carried out in the streets or markets, and also those of domestic workers and those who carried out odd jobs. At the same time, new debts arose for rents, services, previous commit-

---

34 Water shortages were especially frequent in the shantytowns and other low-income neighborhoods during the early months of the pandemic.

ments, food, and cellular phone accounts to connect to school.

With the pandemic, the housing crisis became even more apparent and we saw an increase in land takeovers in the villa itself. Those processes have been led by women with children, women in situations of gender-based violence, young people without a place to live, many who can no longer pay their rents.

Despite the decree banning evictions, there was constant pressure and threats against residents to make them leave their buildings and many evictions did in fact take place, especially in situations of informal housing. We have termed this *"property violence"* and it has been especially intensifying in the informal real estate market, when homes are hotel rooms or rented rooms in a villa, or shared houses in settlements, in which there is not contract or receipt of payment, but the costs and effect of inflation on amounts are equal to or greater than those of renting a small apartment.

Debt seeks to confiscate future income: whether wages promised at the end of the pandemic or state benefits. More directly, people are forced to take out new debts with family and informal circuits. This also becomes a booty for finance companies that are buying debt with the objective of executing the properties in the future. Again, key dilemmas come together in the home: the idea of the home as a "refuge for all" is deromanticized (as the feminist movement has done through emphasis on gender-based violence and exploitation in the household). At the same time, we can verify that a few square meters today costs almost an entire salary (or everything that has to be done to "collect" its equivalent), due to the regulation of the real estate market that allows excessive profits. In turn, this enables an analogy with a global circuit of investment funds that is currently carrying out big business with evictions in different countries around the world.[35]

Property violence is articulated with institutional violence, as shown by a recent study carried out by the sex workers' union AMMAR and researchers from CONICET on the housing situation of sex workers in Buenos Aires' neighborhood of Constitución, where sex workers often rent rooms in hotels or pensions, during the pandemic. They indicate that "the increase in rent prices continued in the hotel-pension market after March 31, 2020, despite presidential decree 320/2020. This accounts for the conditions of greater precarity in that niche of the rental market, characterized by a predominance of informal arrangements."[36]

During the pandemic, institutional, sexist, and property violence were demonstrated as a productive force of real estate extractivism. The case of Bajo Autopista, in Villa 31 and 31 Bis, where the government seeks to drive residents out in order to complete a highway project, was a clear example in this sense.[37] During the pandemic, police

---

35 Myrian Espinoza Minda and Lotta Meri Pirita Tenhunen, *Hasta que caiga el patriarcado y no haya ni un desahucio más. Deuda, vivienda y violencia patriarcal* (Madrid: La Laboratoria y Fundación Rosa Luxemburgo, 2021).

36 Cecilia Inés Varela, Estefania Martynowskyj, Felipe González, Alexandra Sánchez, Maximiliano Albornoz, and Lucía Manes, "Estudio diagnóstico sobre la situación habitacional de las trabajadoras sexuales en el contexto de la pandemia de COVID-19: acceso a la vivienda y violencia institucional en el Barrio de Constitución" (Buenos Aires: CONICET, 2021).

37 The Bajo Autopista land includes all those constructions— housing, businesses, and community spaces—that were built under the Illia Highway, inhabited by 1,300 families. The government of the City of Buenos Aires promised that land to real estate speculators and demolitions have already begun without the necessary permits. The families who live there suffer constant abuse and harassment as a form of disciplining for not agreeing to relocate.

and other state forces explicitly and deliberately abandoned the zone and power outages, robberies, and sexual violence increased. Landfills were created to force families to relocate. Those primarily affected included women, sexual dissidents, and migrants, threatened with deportation.

In September 2020, faced with subjugation, violence, and intimidation in that sector, the Feminist Assembly carried out a march and wheat-pasting campaign with the following slogans: "If the SISU [Secretariat of Social and Urban Integration] abandons us, we organize ourselves," "Neighborhoods free from harassment. Feminist care networks," and "Alive, free, and organized! You are not alone!"

THE CONSOLIDATION OF A SUBJECT OF STRUGGLE: RENTERS

WE DEVELOPED OUR second line of inquiry in political articulation with the tenants' union Inquilinos Agrupados. This organization took on the central task of producing information about the situation of renters across the country given the lack of official data. It carried out its first survey in 2016. In 2020, the worst moment of the pandemic, the issue of debt was incorporated into the survey.

Indebtedness comes to acquire a centrality in renters' situations in the face of greater exposure to threats, pressure, and harassment by property owners. As Inquilinos Agrupados reported, nearly 70 percent of the consultations they receive come from women, primarily heads of households, who have been among those most affected by the housing crisis during the health emergency.

Through organizing, renters were able to demonstrate and put on the public agenda the problematics that are concentrated in homes: debts, rent increases, and evictions.

And, by doing so, they were able to somewhat remove them from their isolation. What they showed was that an ever-greater portion of incomes becomes absorbed by rent. This organizing allowed for the consolidation of renters as political actions, which also showed the transversal character of the housing crisis that no longer only refers solely to low-income sectors and shantytowns, but also includes a large portion of the middle class. At the same time, it highlighted the lack of public policies in relation to that sector and the lack of knowledge about the problems specific to the population of renters.

In August 2019, the National Renters' Federation raised the issue of the need for a freeze on rent prices and, in March 2020, with the arrival of the pandemic, Argentina and several other countries around the world suspended rent increases, as well as evictions. In turn, in June 2020, the "Rent Law" was passed, in the midst of a parliamentary debate over whether or not this issue was part of the health emergency. Among other things, this law included the extension of the contract time to three years, the state's recovery of the capacity to set the rate of increases and the obligation to declare contracts to the Federal Administration of Public Revenue. Property owners and real estate companies, for the most part, have refused to comply with these measures.

This law represents a break with a historical period that started with the last civilian-military dictatorship (1976–1983), in which the state stopped regulating rental prices, and the beginning of the dollarization of the housing market. From that moment on, the market has controlled and decided who can ultimately access housing and who cannot.

This deregulation, furthermore, coincides with a process of "tenantization" of the population. In 2003, 14 percent of the population rented, while in 2020 that number had risen to 19 percent. In the City of Buenos Aires, Ushaia, La Plata, and Rosario, the percentage of renters doubled over that time, reaching 30–40 percent of those cities' populations.[38]

The situation of renters worsened drastically during the pandemic. Gervasio Muñoz draws an analogy with 1870 when yellow fever caused a crisis in the living conditions in crowded tenements, just as the health crisis raised a debate over the completely commodified system of housing access.[39]

The instruction to "Stay at Home" demonstrated the overlaps between the housing crisis and the increase in gender-based violence. The Ni Una Menos Collective, in alliance with Inquilinos Agrupados, proposed the slogan "the home is no place for sexist violence or real estate speculation." That violence, we indicated, materializes in direct abuse by property owners and real estate agents who take advantage of the situation to threaten, harass, not renew contracts, or directly evict renters, despite the decree prohibiting evictions. This situation was even worse for women with children, lesbians, travestis and trans people, translating into direct forms of gender-based violence. The increase in situations of gender-based violence that was triggered in the months of confinement became another element of housing precarization.

One unavoidable question that appears today is: who owns the houses and hotels that primarily evict women, lesbians, travestis, and trans people? The imperative to Stay at Home as a protective formula was shown to not be so

---

38 Fernando Muñoz, *La desigualdad bajo techo* (Buenos Aires: Ciccus, 2020).

39 Luci Cavallero and Gervasio Muñoz, "Alquileres: aumentos, deudas y miedo al desalojo" *Página/12* (August 1, 2021), https://www.pagina12.com.ar/358144-alquileres-aumentos-deudas-y-miedo-al-desalojo.

simple, or effective, for everyone to follow. The measures adopted by the government, such as the IFE, along with the prohibition of evictions and rent freeze, sought to respond to that situation in the short term. However, evictions continued to occur, demonstrating the lack of mechanisms to force compliance with the prohibition, and the subsidy only lasted for three months. The increase in debt to pay rent shaped situations of violence that multiplied with the pandemic.

Data from September 2021 shows that approximately 50 percent of households that rent have debts, demonstrating that they prioritize paying rent and take out debt in order to live.[40] Being a renter today is to be indebted. Being indebted means being obligated to more precarious forms of work and, during the pandemic, an increase in domestic violence is added to the gendered violence of abuse by property owners.

Debt is the prelude to eviction and, in turn, the way to postpone it. For many people, being left without a place to live means directly living on the streets or returning to violent households from which they had managed to escape. For many, it implies burdening family members and creating situations of greater overcrowding and precarity.

The renters' organization has posed political problems that need to be addressed: how can we politicize rental prices? How can we connect real estate rent with financial rent? What types of businesses in the city depend on the pauperization of renters? Going further, they also ask: what political alliances are necessary between rural and urban renters, and between renters on the formal and informal

---

40 "La mayoría de los inquilinos destina entre un tercio y la mitad de sus ingresos a pagar el alquiler," *Télam* (September 22, 2021), www.telam.com.ar/notas/202109/569430-encuesta-inquilinos-argentina-ingresos-alquileres.html.

market? How can we organize and scale up the conflict if we don't know who owns the property?

At the same time, resistance to the housing crisis took on a global character and new vocabularies of struggle appeared for thinking about the issue of rent in connection to feminism, the defense of human rights, and environmental movements. In this sense, the connection between the dynamics of the housing crisis and the economy of violence in cities, which especially impacts feminized and racialized populations, became clear.

The transnational dimension of the problematic also resulted in a pluralization of forms of action and strategies. Some of these strategies were oriented toward the legal plane (laws prohibiting evictions, rent regulation, demand for the cancellation of debts accumulated during the pandemic). Yet others included direct confrontation such as rent strikes, campaigns against investment funds, the creation of groups to warn of and resist evictions, and educational campaigns to inform renters about their special rights during the pandemic.[41]

THE HOME AS A LABORATORY OF CAPITAL

WE WANT TO delve into some of our theoretical arguments and more concretely explain how the home has become a battlefield, a place of multiple labors, a space of new uses from which the platform economy benefits, a site in which domestic debts and financial technology lands. It is funda-

---

41 See Inquilinos Agrupados, "Encuentro Internacional de Organizaciones Inquilinas" [video], streamed live on September 23, 2021), https://www.youtube.com/watch?v=bv0YI638Lnc.

mental, as we pointed out, to be able to problematize what happens there, at home, which is flush with our daily life. It is the feminist movement that has deconfined that place that, for a long time, capital attempted to keep *private, family-based and a privileged surface of unpaid work.*

When we say that the home has been transformed into a favored site of experimentation for capital, we are not arguing that it is a closed or finished process. That is one important insight of our feminist methodology: in that vital space of the home, we see an open dispute and not definitive modifications. Even so, we cannot but start from the changes that have *already occurred* in many domestic routines, in labor dynamics, in the very marks imposed by the pandemic's reorganization of the sensible and of logistics.

In this way, in this work, we argue that the home—its spatiality, functioning, and dynamics—suffered from nodal reconfigurations during these two years that have not ended with the end of the period of health restriction measures. In the home then, three simultaneous processes are combined:

1) Processes of the *intrusion* of financial technology within homes. As we have noted, feminism has long fought against the idea of the home as a refuge, showing how it is a space of interconnected oppressions and dynamics of exploitation. Domestic work has also been conceptualized in opposition to the idea of the home as a space of the private and the peaceful, isolated from the logics of the labor market.

But now there is one most step that we want to emphasize: households are suffering the direct intrusion of financial technology (fintech). In other words: new financial technologies take homes as a target and favored landing zone. In this case, we are referring to mobile payment platforms, electronic wallets, and digital banks. These have been channels for taking out credit, payments, transfers, and investment, that have been incorporated into an everyday life that assumes the practicality of the virtual, which was initially accelerated by the social distancing measures.

The private fintech companies primarily target their services at a bankarized population of which 62 percent are beneficiaries of welfare programs and 28 percent receive pension payments, according to data from Argentinian Republic Central Bank's Report on Financial Inclusion. In other words, prior to the health emergency, the expansion of financial technologies targeting the most precarious sectors was becoming an accelerator for taking out non-banking debt. This in turn was made possible by the expansion of digital infrastructure (basically, cellphones) in the sectors with the fewest resources as the necessary condition for so-called financial inclusion. The whole phenomenon reaches an unthinkable speed and scale in the face of the restrictions on physical presence imposed by the quarantine and turns into a particularly agile way for accelerating indebtedness due to the intensification of the crisis of incomes.

The Argentine government decided[42] that private companies providing fintech services would not be allowed to provide the means for distributing the emergency subsidies, since in the previous months it had been verified that they were charging very high interest rates on the loans they offered.[43] In fact, there were complaints about the compulsory withdrawals of debts with banks from the

---

42 Andrea Catalano, "La ANSES dejó afuera del pago de la IFE a las billeteras virtuales: vuelven a ganar los bancos y el efectivo," *Iprofesional* (April 16, 2020), www.iprofesional.com/economia/313935-por-que-la-anses-dejo-afuera-del-pago-de-la-ife-a-las-billeteras-virtuales.

43 "Otro golpe del Banco Central a las fintech: cuáles son las acusaciones contra las prestamistas digitales," *IProUP* (June 20, 2020), https://www.iproup.com/finanzas/14419-prestamos-fintech-que-tasas-excesivas-encontro-el-banco-central.

emergency subsidy itself.[44] This exclusion of private banks corresponded with two state-owned banks offering virtual wallets to access the subsidy.

Here we see an open dispute between private financial technology companies and public banks over the inclusion of this newly available population, which is also a key point for the political management of the crisis.[45] Specifically, Banco Provincia's DNI Account and Banco Nacion's BNA, which were the key mechanisms for receiving the emergency benefits during the pandemic. After two years of the pandemic, the fintech companies have been consolidated as the most chosen platforms for taking out one's first credit

---

44 "Denuncian a bancos por aplicar descuentos sobre el bono de $10000," *BAE Negocios* (May 10, 2020), www.baenegocios. com/economia/Denuncian-a-bancos-por-descuentos-en-el-bono-de-10000-20200510-0036.html.

45 The Central Bank of the Argentine Republic began regulating the activity of payment service provider (PSP) in January 2020, through Communication A #6859, in which fintech were prohibited from investing with their clients' funds, since "all accounts must be visible, in pesos, in financial entities in the country and always immediately available upon request, for an amount at least equivalent to that credited to the payment account." The regulation continues, saying "PSP may, at the request of their clients, apply the balance of payment accounts in common money funds and will be required to report the invested balances separately from the rest." Later, in Communication A #6885, also in January, said companies were urged to register and fall under the supervision of the Superintendency of Financial Entities. On March 11, a significant milestone occurred in relation to the advance of virtual wallets when the Labor Ministry repealed a resolution from 2018 that allowed employers to pay wages through mobile devices and other enabled electronic devices. According to Resolution 179/2020, "Enabling the payment of remuneration through virtual wage accounts implies placing workers, as well as employers, in a state of defenselessness" (September 2020 Report on the Promotion of Policies of Gender, Safeguarding Respect, and Labor Coexistence).

line, showing that they are a privileged channel for new debts. With this, it becomes clear that the pandemic has served as a *financial laboratory* and has traced a new set of corridors and channels through which finance excavates new circuits of value extraction. To the forms of digital-financial intrusion (none of which are imaginable without the use of cellular phones), we should add the use, from homes, of delivery platforms. These platforms also underwent a boom during the pandemic and have connected precaritized domestic spaces with services that are provided through cheap logistics and precarious labor conditions.

2) Processes of the intensification of unpaid domestic labor to respond to the necessities of the health, food, and housing crises; both in households and in neighborhoods and community spaces, as well as in response to the lack of public resources to guarantee social reproduction. The decline in paid work (especially that linked to popular economies and street economies, and, particularly, for domestic employees) due to the crisis and the devaluation of incomes due to inflation have led to a substantial drop in income. This occurred at the same time as an increase in work, especially unpaid work. This increase in the burden of unpaid care work has affected women's opportunities, especially for female heads of households responsible for children, to participate in the labor market. Thus, the pandemic has especially penalized those households through the increase in care work, restrictions to accessing public education services, and the lack of time to access the labor market.

Care tasks, accessing scarce (health) services, and, in some places, replacing services due to the suspension and/or virtualization of the public (for example, children's schooling) have intensified and extended the workday in the home, especially for women, lesbians, travestis, and trans women. Thus, the "way out" of the pandemic has strongly modified routines and workloads. Tele-work, care work, managing purchases to cushion price increases due to inflation, managing requests for state benefits, and, above all, ever more precarious conditions for sustaining the reproduction of life overlap in multiple, simultaneous working days.

Here we can point to the reinforcement of gender mandates that are knotted together in this moment of crisis under forms of *superexploitation*. Superexploitation, returning to Mies, is defined by the fact that capital not only appropriates from surplus labor and time in respect to "necessary" labor (that is, surplus value), but it also advances over the appropriation of the time and labor necessary for the production of subsistence.[46] This is an important interpretative key for thinking about what new configurations between production and reproduction are being disputed today and how they are translated in the very space of the household.

3) Processes of the "production" of new debts as the result of the fixation of unpaid tasks, the devaluation of incomes, women leaving the workforce, and the increase in prices for basic inputs for reproduction: food and housing. In this way, we see a circuit: not only do new financial technologies—which are directly connected to the financial market—interfere in the home, but also the intensification of unpaid labor in the home makes it necessary to take out new debts. The situation is paradoxical: the burden of greater unpaid reproductive work is compounded by greater household debt. Dynamics that started during the quarantine but continue to this day in different ways, can be understood from the perspective of which movements generate debts and which generate rents. This method allows for showing who can stay at home and who cannot, and that moving about or staying at home has dif-

---

46 Mies, *Patriarchy and Global Accumulation*.

ferential effects in terms of incomes and debts. Thus, we see how debt functions in a concrete way as a mechanism of discipline and value extraction during the crisis and how housing operates as a strategic spatiality of these disputes.

To understand these issues, we must enter into dialogue with those debates emphasizing rethinking domestic spatiality expanded to territories that are not reduced to the household and in connection with debts that make it so that housing, as we said, is a spatiality directly connected to global financial flows. To the price of housing itself, household indebtedness must be added. The type of situation diversified and increased during the pandemic as "non-banking" debts for rent and electricity, water, gas, and Internet services grew at an accelerated pace. This situation was assembled with a prior reality of household indebtedness, especially of the most precarious household, as we have analyzed in earlier works.

CONCLUSIONS

WE HAVE TRIED to contribute to the visibilization of social reproduction as a strategic sphere. Because key reconfigurations took place there during the pandemic that included an intensification of reproductive work: if there are no or few day cares, health services, and water providers, it will be the neighborhood and community arrangements and the work of women, lesbians, travestis, and trans persons that will replace them. Because, household indebtedness meshes with social reproduction, placing quick monetary solutions to the increasing cost of daily life and emergencies that are no longer exceptional. In fact, channelized finance *in* homes and energized *from* homes reshape what we understand by domestic space. A key issue is articulated around social reproduction: housing policy, today a central part of real estate and financial speculation; and new financial technologies land in households themselves and become part of daily life. Additionally, we have sought to highlight how the violence of debt concentrated on attacking the stability of access to housing produces a specific exercise of sovereignty in the territory by finance.

In this way, explaining why there is a change in the relations of production that takes the sphere of reproduction (violently attacked and made "unsafe") a privileged site becomes a central hypothesis for understanding the ways in which care and telework, the restriction of incomes and emergence of new debts, greater difficulties in formal and informal employment and the housing emergency become mixed together, along with the strengthening of platforms as service providers and the increase in internet and telephone rates.

As we pointed out, many informal workers, especially those involved in the popular economy and different forms of self-employment, as well as household workers and formal workers who lost their jobs, very quickly saw their incomes drastically reduced, which particularly affected the renting population. Missed payments added up for rents and basic services, in the form of new debts. Or debt was taken out to not miss a payment and thus avoid eviction. The economic violence that is expressed in housing access and its connection with gender violence has only accelerated with the pandemic, putting the domestic space understood as "home" in the spotlight.

Drawing on what we have said before, it becomes clear that there is a new push of what we call *property violence* due to the fact that property is rendered visible as the border that each conflict crosses in the pandemic. It is not always that clear-cut, but now the discussion appears focused on the territories of social reproduction—food, housing, land, education, and health: spaces that have been made visible as fundamental by feminisms—and over the command of future labor that household indebtedness seeks to control.

It is no coincidence then that the housing crisis is one of the most salient features of the pandemic. The home, that supposed space of private refuge, denounced by feminisms as the epicenter of violence, is transformed in a terminal of flows that are a central part of the global political and economic scene in the crisis. The "property violence" that has been exacerbated during the pandemic (property rights and patents, forms of "lordship" to use Rita Segato's formulation) is a reaction that precisely expresses a proprietary power that, faced with the emergency demands pushed from below (the food and housing crises, for example) sees itself threatened in terms of what it considers its "natural right" of possession.

The battlefield of capital against life plays out today over the terrain of reproduction, over the remuneration of so-called *essential* work and our collective capacity to attack the extraction of rents and modify tax structures. This battlefield is not abstract. It is made up of each struggle in the crisis, each concrete initiative. The challenge is to connect the demands that emerge from diverse territories and transform them into a future horizon in the here and now.

2. COUNTER-CARTOGRAPHIES OF DOMESTIC TERRITORIES

WHAT HAS THE pandemic taught us about the spatiality of social and material reproduction and the home? And, what methods enable us to address this question, in all its complexity, without reproducing the perspective of capital? As stated earlier, we are particularly interested in debates that recognize *domestic territories* that extend beyond the home and, through a focus on debt, understanding how those territories are directly connected to global financial flows. When we say that the home served as a laboratory during the pandemic, we are also saying that the very spatiality of the home is itself under dispute.

We can start from an initial question: where are domestic territories? How far do they reach and how are they connected to other spatialities? Then, how are those domestic territories structured? We can ask, who maintains them and how? What relationships of power and control, of solidarity and alliance take place within them? What subjectivities are shaped there? The home emerges as a central site, but in connection with many others. The nuclear family appears as one form of its reproduction, but not the only one. We can see the state's changing and sometimes contradictory role. We can see how finance has become more and more intertwined in different aspects of these domestic territories, creating direct pathways to other spatialities and other scales.

Our line of questioning opens up an immediately political register. It reminds us of what we have already known: that the terrain of reproduction is necessary for the maintenance of capitalism as a social relation but also for the reproduction of life itself. It points to the political importance of reproduction as a terrain that capital seeks to colonize. There is a fundamental spatial element to this battle. We cannot remain trapped in the home, nor can our analysis. Deconfining what happens in the home is the first step to politicizing it, to finding collective solutions instead of remaining trapped in sensations of private guilt and political impotence. Mapping the expanded circuits of reproduction allows us to more fully comprehend who bears the costs of social reproduction and who reaps the benefits. And it shows us where we can interrupt the reproduction of capitalist relations and how we can create relations of reproduction otherwise.

FEMINIST COUNTER-MAPPING AS METHOD

WHERE ARE THESE domestic territories that extend beyond individual homes? Who inhabits them and labors within them? How do they exist in connection with other spaces and spatialities? Here a feminist counter-mapping has emerged as a useful tool for understanding, locating, and intervening in this expanded geography of reproduction. As a methodology, feminist counter-cartography prioritizes situated and embodied knowledges, inviting subjects as participants to map their own lived experiences, bodily sensations and emotions, and territorial relationships. These counter-maps, premised on relationality, are also just as concerned with connections and relations between different experiences and conflicts, between different body-territories and their struggles. In other words, starting from concrete bodies and situations then allowing for mapping broader territories, for mapping the whole, but from a situated perspective.

This feminist counter-mapping offers an alternative to traditional, patriarchal forms of cartography. Rather than producing a vision from above, a God's-eye view claiming to be all-seeing and all-encompassing, a masculinist and patriarchal perspective, feminist counter-maps recognize the situatedness of all perspectives and privileges those of marginalized and feminized subjects. For us, feminist counter-mapping is both a practical research method that allows us to explore extended domestic territories without predetermined notions of their geographic confines and, at the same time, a tool for intervening in that territoriality, producing geographies of social reproduction otherwise. Maps, we know, act on the world. They are not mere representations of what exists, but call into being ways of inhabiting and relating to the territory. Property lines and borders, drawn on maps, are imposed on territories, backed by state violence; routes suggested by GPS create new traffic patterns, privileging certain methods and modes of transportation above others. Historically, and today, cartography has been a foundational element of colonial and imperialist projects, a way of claiming territories and inflicting violence. Feminist counter-cartographies can, instead, open up other ways not only of seeing and representing the world, but also of being in and with the world.[1]

Starting from specific situations, specific bodies, territories, and conflicts, this feminist counter-mapping puts a feminist epistemology into practice when it comes to mapping, recognizing the positionality and situatedness of those making the maps. Used as a research methodology, feminist counter-mapping can engage the whole range of participants' senses, sensations, sensibilities, affects, and emotions. It does not privilege the larger scale over the smaller scales of the body, household, and community, but rather is able to incorporate how multiple scales intersect and overlap in our everyday lives. These feminist counter-maps push and challenge conventional understandings of what even counts as a map, for example including different types of artistic elements, or expanding and diversifying what is considered *data* worth including on the map. Feminist counter-mapping projects have thus focused on users' experiences and feelings in public services or the sensations of crossing borders, as well as the spatiality of violences or sensations of safety and lack of safety, to name a few.[2]

---

1 For work on the history and conceptualization of counter-mapping, see Craig Dalton and Liz Mason-Deese, "Counter (Mapping) Actions: Mapping as Militant Research," *ACME: An International E-Journal for Critical* Geographies 11, no. 3 (2012); or Liz Mason-Deese, "Critical Cartography," in *International Encyclopedia of Human Geography*, Second Edition, ed. Audrey Kobayashi (Amsterdam: Elsevier, 2020), 423–432. For a wide range of examples of counter-mapping, see: *This Is Not an Atlas*, https://notanatlas.org/book/.

2 For more on some of the concepts behind feminist counter-mapping, see: Catherine D'Ignazio and Lauren F. Klein, *Data Feminism* (Cambridge, MA: MIT Press, 2020); Bianca Fileborn, "Digital Mapping as Feminist Method: Critical Reflections," *Qualitative Research*, 23, no. 2 (2023): 343–361; Meghan

From another angle, Indigenous communities and feminist organizations have elaborated the concept of the body-territory as a way of encapsulating an ontological unity between body-territory beyond any notions of individual ownership and property. This perspective highlights the ongoing relationship between processes of colonization of territory and the constitution of patriarchy and sexist violence. As a premise for counter-mapping, a wide range of feminist, community, and Indigenous collectives and organizations have deployed the concept of body-territory as a research-intervention tool to address a variety of problematics from the effects of oil extraction or mining on the body-territory to elaborating notions of community wellness. By inviting participants to map the impact of different processes on their body-territories, including material impacts, feelings, sensations, and so on, this body-territory mapping creates a collective understanding of contemporary dynamics, explicitly linking the scale of the body with other scales.[3]

Feminist counter-maps thus create room for a multiplicity of voices and experiences, without creating hierarchies among them. There is room for all of us on the map. These counter-maps thus start from a recognition and valuing of difference and of particular body-territories. Yet they do not stop there. The counter-map must also create its mark on its world and, in this case, it does so by creating a common

---

Kelly, "Mapping Syrian Refugee Border Crossings: A Feminist Approach" *Cartographic Perspectives*, no. 93 (2019): 34–64.

3 Practices of body-territory mapping are quite common among community and feminist organizations. For one in-depth examination of these processes, see: Colectivo Miradas Críticas del Territorio desde el Feminismo, *Mapeando el cuerpo-territorio. Guía metodológica para mujeres que defienden sus territorios* (Quito: CLACSO, 2017).

ground, possibilities for connection and alliance, identifying shared struggles and demands. As a necessarily collective process, feminist counter-mapping begins to create those alliances in its very process.

Our feminist counter-mapping of domestic territories during the pandemic thus incorporates different perspectives and elements at diverse scales, providing a complex and more complete map of the extent of domestic territories and also producing alliances to intervene in those territories. We map the effects of the pandemic and quarantine measures on bodies and their territories. We have mapped where we—women, lesbians, trans and nonbinary people—went and did not go during the pandemic, where and who carried out different types of labor and for whom, where our money goes, and our support networks and alliances: the expanded domestic territories that make our survival possible. We make our maps in assembly, whether in person or virtual, as ways of sharing and building collective knowledge, identifying common problems, pinpointing possible sites of resistance, and strengthening our support networks.[4]

---

4 For example, in a related project, the Counter-Cartographies Collective asked participants questions such as: "Whose labor sustains your quarantine? Whose quarantine does your labor sustain?" And, to push thoughts toward resistance in the framework of the feminist strike: "What would it take to make your strike possible? We know we cannot strike alone. We know that the care work we do is vitally necessary, and yet, we *must* strike. Could you *imagine* a map of connections, support, the infrastructure, that would make your strike possible?" See https://www.countercartographies.org/map-your-feminist-strike/.

UNDERSTANDING GEOGRAPHIES OF SOCIAL REPRODUCTION

WE START OUR inquiry from the premise that the spatiality of reproduction is itself a terrain of struggle. Feminist geographers have tracked the shifting spatialities of social reproduction over time and place, showing that they are anything but natural. Instead, they are the result of gendered power differentials and struggles. Where social reproduction takes place is intimately tied to questions of who bears the costs and responsibility for that labor, as well as who makes the decisions over *how* reproduction takes place, what exactly it is that is being reproduced.

The spatial separation, the enclosure and privatization of reproduction, is a fundamental element of both the emergence of capitalism and the construction of the modern gender binary.[5] Maintaining that spatial separation, especially through the further privatization of reproduction, thus continues to play an essential role in the maintenance of gendered exploitation and hierarchies. The relegation of certain tasks to the household—their enclosure in private "non-political" space occurs simultaneously with the devaluation of those tasks and the people who carry them out. In opposition, feminist perspectives have argued for the recognition of the significance of the space of the household and the work carried out there.

---

5 Silvia Federici, *Caliban and the Witch: Women, the Body, and Primitive Accumulation* (Brooklyn: Autonomedia, 2004); Maria Mies, *Patriarchy and Accumulation on a World Scale: Women in the International Division of Labour* (London: Zed Books, 1986).

The spatiality of reproduction, however, is not limited to the household. Perspectives that focus on the geographies of reproduction beyond the Western Global North, and beyond white middle- and upper-class families, have especially highlighted the role of different forms of community, institutions, and the state in reproduction. A geographic perspective complicates the cartography of social reproduction by recognizing the specificity of structures and models of social reproduction in distinct places: recognizing that enclosure in the household as a housewife has primarily been the experience of white women of a certain class and that at different places and time, the state and community have taken on greater or lesser responsibility for social reproduction. In other words, what is necessary for social reproduction varies across time and space, as does how that social reproduction is organized. Centering agricultural work, work in the community, or work in the "informal sector," thus substantially alters our understanding of the geographies both of social reproduction and production and shows that women have always been engaged in both productive and reproductive work. This again demonstrates that the spatial confinement of reproduction is anything but natural, but rather should be seen as an open field of struggle.

Geographers have specifically highlighted the spatial and embodied nature of social reproduction and the geopolitics and relational scales of social reproduction, highlighting the co-production of everyday practices and larger social, economic, and political structures.[6] In other words, it is not a matter of an opposition between a *micro* and a *macro* perspective, but a perspective that grasps the

6 Vivian Rodríguez-Rocha, "Social Reproduction Theory: State of the Field and New Directions in Geography," *Geography Compass* 15, no. 8 (2021).

intimate intertwining of different scales. Indeed, while economic and political processes at larger scales shape and condition everyday spaces, it is also precisely in those spaces of the home, the neighborhood, and the community where social relations are made and unmade.

Here reproduction can refer to something much broader than either the reproduction of the labor force or the reproduction of the capitalist social relation but can also refer to the reproduction of life itself. This perspective includes the reproduction and maintenance of the physical environment and environmental resources necessary to guarantee both that production and life continue. Amaia Pérez Orozco, drawing on feminist economics and Spanish and Latin American feminist movements, specifically proposes "putting life in the center" of both our analysis and political action: evaluating policies and structures based on their capacity to sustain life as a whole and building structures that enable a life worth living for all.[7] Going further, the aforementioned concept of body-territory points to another way of understanding scale and interdependence, recognizing that bodies and territories cannot be reproduced independently of one another.

Thus, a focus on the geography of social reproduction points to its complexity, defying easy binaries between production and reproduction. This focus on the materiality and spatiality of reproduction allows for recognizing how the spheres of production and reproduction overlap, through the commodification of many of the activities of reproduction, women performing waged work at home, the hiring of other women to carry out work of social reproduction, and practices of consumption, among others.

---

7 Amaia Pérez Orozco, *The Feminist Subversion of the Economy: Contributions for Life against Capital*, trans. Liz Mason-Deese (Brooklyn and Philadelphia: Common Notions, 2022).

Proposing what they term "life's work," Mitchell, Marston, and Katz directly challenge these binaries, arguing "If . . . social reproduction is about how we as subjects live at and outside of work, then the categorical binaries of state and society, work and home, production and social reproduction cannot be maintained."[8] More recently, Pirone, examining how the COVID-19 pandemic has transformed geographies of both production and reproduction, argues: "The house becomes *oikos*—a hybrid place of production and reproduction, smart working and family care—but also the boundary line of social distance between the self and others, between what is ours and what is not."[9] In other words, detailed attention to the material practices of reproduction defy simple binaries pointing to the need for a much more complex cartography of where and how reproduction is organized.

It is in this sense that feminist geography provides crucial insights into the spatiality of value production, going beyond the confines of officially recognized workplaces to recognize the multiplicity of sites of exploitation and value extraction. Mezzadri, again shifting the focus of labor geographies to the Global South and processes of labor informalization, draws on the work of feminist geographers to propose a "value theory of inclusion" that recognizes how social reproduction contributes to the generation of value. This theory is based on a decentering of wages and prices in economic analysis, the recognition of the multiplicity of forms of exploitation, and the recognition of the

---

8 Katharyne Mitchell, Sallie Marston, and Cindi Katz, eds., *Life's Work: Geographies of Social Reproduction* (Oxford: Blackwell Publishers, 2003), 433.

9 Maurilio Pirone, "Pandemic Transition: Techno-Politics and Social Reproduction Struggles," *Human Geography* 14, no. 2 (2021): 289.

"interpenetration between production and reproduction in processes of value-generation."[10] This perspective builds on and expands on those calling for wages for housework in the 1970s, recognizing the variety of forms and spaces of feminized labor and their contributions.

Continuing our examination of the expansion of geographies of reproduction, we must look at the spatial implications of the financialization of social reproduction. Debt has particularly affected the spatiality of social reproduction through the externalization and financialization of many aspects of social reproduction and finance's entrance into the household. Finance has entered the realm of everyday life, transforming intimate social relations in the process. Financialization also implies a geographic transfer of risk into the private household and encourages households to think, to make decisions and operate, as financial entities.[11] Yet, we are wary of perspectives that solely focus on the impacts of finance on the household, casting households and their members as victims to international financial institutions and flows, rather than active agents producing value and resisting exploitation.

However, by pointing out the historical and geographical construction of the gendered separation between reproduction and production, feminist geography also highlights struggles in the field of social reproduction and

---

10 Alessandra Mezzadri, "A Value Theory of Inclusion: Informal Labour, the Homeworker, and the Social Reproduction of Value," *Antipode* 53, no. 4 (2021): 1194.

11 For geographic perspectives on this financialization, see Manuel B. Aalbers, "Financialization," in *The International Encyclopedia of Geography: People, the Earth, Environment, and Technology*, ed. D. Richardson, N. Castree, M.F. Goodchild, A.L. Kobayashi and R. Marston (Oxford: Wiley, 2019); and Desiree Fields, "Unwilling Subjects of Financialization," *International Journal of Urban and Regional Research* 41, no. 4 (2017): 588–603.

allows for imagining reproduction otherwise. As Norton and Katz eloquently state: "The form and content of social reproduction, as much as the means of its provision, are forged through struggle, making it a contradictory realm of both the continuation of capitalist social relations and the possibility of their transformation."[12] Contemporary feminist movements precisely aim to intervene in these contested geographies of reproduction, not only challenging the uneven distribution of reproductive labor and where that labor occurs, but also what exactly is being reproduced and how.

THE HOME SPILLS OVER

ONE OF THE principal achievements of the feminist movement in Argentina in recent years has been precisely to challenge the confinement and privatization of social reproduction in the home. It inherits this struggle from a long legacy of movements, both feminist and others, that have challenged the privatization of social reproduction and also aimed to carry out social reproduction differently. These range from movements seeking to increase the state's responsibility for social reproduction, defending public education, health care, and housing, to organizations that directly take reproduction into their own hands, creating their own schools, clinics, housing cooperatives, etc.

In Argentina, the struggles of unemployed workers and workers of the popular economy have played a key role in this regard. The unemployed who blockaded roads, highways, and bridges in protest of the effects of mass

---

12 Jack Norton and Cindi Katz, "Social Reproduction," *The International Encyclopedia of Geography* (2017): 1.

unemployment on their lives were organizing, more than anything, in response to a crisis of social reproduction. Faced with the inability to pay basic utilities or afford rising food costs due to income loss, the unemployed began collectively organizing in their own neighborhoods. Were they organizing in their living spaces because they had lost access to "real" workplaces? Or was this form of organization a way of recognizing and organizing around the "life's work" centered in household and community spaces? In any case, the efforts of the unemployed workers' organizations began to focus more and more on issues of social reproduction and, importantly, creating their own autonomous forms of reproduction: health clinics and schools, urban gardening and farming, childcare and housing cooperatives.[13]

Yet, of course none of this is new: as discussed above, Indigenous and peasant communities, to name a few, those on the margins of the world economy, have long managed their material reproduction beyond or underneath the capitalist economy. Here the borders of the domestic are more porous and fluid, expanding into the neighborhood and community, constantly challenging its confinement. What makes these contemporary movements noteworthy is how they explicitly seek to challenge capital's confinement of reproduction in the household and the devaluing of that work and make reorganizing reproduction a central task.

Again, in popular economies, especially those marked by the experiences of economic crisis and grassroots

---

13 For more on the unemployed workers' movements, see Colectivo Situaciones and the MTD of Solano, *Hypothesis 891: Beyond the Roadblocks*, trans. Dina Khorasanee and Liz Mason-Deese (London: Minor Compositions, 2023). For writing on the unemployed workers' movements precisely as a struggle over social reproduction, see Liz Mason-Deese, "Unemployed Workers' Movements and the Territory of Social Reproduction," *Journal of Resistance Studies* 2, no. 2 (2017): 65–99.

organizing of the unemployed and others, we have seen that the geographies of social reproduction necessarily expand beyond the household and the nuclear family. Women run day cares out of their homes because of the lack of public or even affordable options, community-run soup kitchens fill in the gaps and become essential as inflation makes basic food items inaccessible to many. Community run health clinics not only provide basic health care services in underserved neighborhoods, but also run programs and interventions specifically on problematics of those communities: from drug use to mosquito-borne illnesses to gender-based violence to basic nutrition. Unemployed workers' organizations and other community groups have taken over or purchased land and built their own housing cooperatives that not only directly address the issue of housing but are also spatially designed to center and collectivize reproductive tasks, including collective kitchens and child-care spaces.

Thus, we see that these movements, both through necessity and then, increasingly, through an explicitly feminist analysis not only called for but put into practice a social reorganization of reproduction. This involved opening up the domestic sphere—both in discursive terms and in practical terms—talking about what goes on at home, making it the object of political discussion and intervention, and taking tasks that were often confined to the private sphere out into public, collectivizing them. This also necessarily led to a questioning of traditional gender roles and hierarchies: when "women's work" is taken out of the home, then is it no longer "women's work"? When women's work is no longer considered the least important, but rather central to a movement's agenda, then what does that do to gender hierarchies? Is it perhaps these shifts—in the spatiality of reproductive activity and in gender hierarchies—that has triggered the intense conservative backlash in recent years?

STAY AT HOME

IN THE PANDEMIC, this spatiality of reproduction is precisely what came under dispute as capital perhaps saw an opportunity to fix reproduction in the home, to break down the expanded networks of reproduction, to more efficiently control and extract value from that reproductive labor. At the same time, formal and informal, networks, alliances, and organizations of women, lesbians, travestis, and trans people have constantly adapted to the changing situation, continuing to challenge the enclosure of reproduction in the household, even under new circumstances.

What did "Stay at Home" orders mean for the geography of social reproduction? It meant that, suddenly, bodies and labors were fixed, confined to the home. Many types of formally recognized employment—if they could be carried out virtually—moved into the household. But, more than anything, it was a confinement of social reproduction to the household and the nuclear family: schooling, cooking, childcare, care of the sick and elderly, even leisure and entertainment. It meant a reworking of interior spaces: bedrooms turned into offices, living rooms turned into daycares, kitchens turned into schools. And it also involved a discursive re-confinement: the home is now, suddenly, considered the safest space. Safe for whom? What does that mean for all the women and LGBTTQI+ people who continue to be most unsafe precisely in their homes? What is made invisible by the discourse of the safety of the home?

How can a specifically feminist counter-mapping render visible what has happened to the home during the pandemic? One strand of this cartography starts from the question of labor, understood, of course, in its broad sense, to map where, when, and by whom re/productive work is being carried out. This opens the home up again, recognizing it as a site of multiple forms of labor and, crucially, allows us to see the relationships between these different forms of labor. A later step allows us to see who is benefiting from that labor and how value is being extracted. Where does all of our money go? To pay rent and utilities, to access food and medical care, an assortment of apps to make life and childcare easier under quarantine, to pay for entertainment and communication, etc. Our mapping thus points to the financialization of the home during the pandemic and how the home becomes directly connected to globalized financial flows through new financial technologies from banking apps and digital wallets to a whole myriad of different platforms.

As new financial technologies take root in the household, it is impossible (as it perhaps always was) to speak of the home as isolated, as a somehow separate domain from the places of production. During the pandemic, then, the home became a laboratory for new forms of value extraction, making the centrality of the household clearer than ever. This occurred in two senses: first, as many types of formally recognized work were moved into the home under work from home schemes. In that move, many of the costs associated with that work were shifted onto the worker as well, for example, paying electricity, Internet, and other utility bills. Second, reproductive labor intensified in the home due to the lack of public and collective forms of addressing reproduction during the pandemic: childcare, education, cooking, cleaning, and maintaining the space all became the responsibility of the individual members of the household and, more likely than not, women in those households. Occurring simultaneously, these dynamics mean an intensification of multiple forms of labor in the same space, at the same time, both increasing rates of super-exploitation and remaking the internal space of the home. Meanwhile, to make up for inflation and income loss during the pandemic, households turn to credit to pay for everything from their Internet bill to groceries. Debts begin to add up.

Mapping these debts then allows us to map the new forms of value extraction that directly target the home. Debts to pay for food, utilities, education, and health care extract value from social reproduction itself, becoming completely divorced from any necessary connection with formal or waged labor. It is also in this sense that the boundaries between "production" and "reproduction" are blurred, and the home becomes a central site for understanding contemporary capitalism as a whole.

MAPPING LINES OF STRUGGLE

THE PRIVATIZATION AND confinement of reproduction in the home, at the same time, reinforces both a heteropatriarchal notion of the family and a neoliberal subjectivity, in which each household is responsible for itself. In the pandemic, mainstream discourse quickly shifted from one of collective care and safety to one of individual responsibility: each person or household was responsible for calculating their own risks, if you got sick, it was your own fault. Never mind the enormous differences in capacity to mitigate risks and bear the costs of staying home.

At the same time, the hardening of the nuclear family with stay-at-home orders also, in many cases, meant a re-entrenchment of traditional gender roles within the household. As reproductive labor in the home intensified, so too did a conventional gendered distribution of labor, in which women took on the majority of that reproductive work. During the pandemic, women were significantly more likely than men to leave the paid workforce, in large part due to the extra reproductive work they were responsible for in the home. As a result, patriarchal relations and hierarchies were reinforced in the home as paid labor continues to be recognized and valued above all other types of work.

Adding to this scenario, debt, as has already been pointed out from many different directions, functions not only as a form of value extraction, but also a form of discipline. Debt serves to ensure obedience, both in the present and in the future, to ensure that labor is not refused, to ensure that the indebted organize their lives around repaying their debt and nothing else. This takes on an especially gendered aspect in forms of credit that are specifically targeted to women, based on notions of women as willing to sacrifice themselves to be good citizens and caregivers. Thus, debt is intimately tied to gender mandates, producing not only indebted subjects but indebted subjects according to heteropatriarchal norms. When debt lands in the terrain of social reproduction, this dynamic is intensified, as debt is taken out to fulfill feminized duties in the household. Thus, financial capital's assault on and colonization of the terrain of social reproduction can also be seen as an attempt to intervene in the production of subjectivity that occurs there. Not only is value extracted from the home, but, at the same time, an indebted and gendered subjectivity is produced.

Yet, social reproduction, itself, is already a site of struggle: capitalist social reproduction reproduces the capitalist social relation and people as workers. However, that social reproduction is itself never complete, there is always spillover and lines of flight. The movements we have spoken of—from feminist movements to tenants' unions to unemployed workers' movements—however, also carry out reproduction otherwise, to (re)produce other social relations and other subjectivities. They have opened space for more collective understandings of life and the responsibility for maintaining it, collectivizing reproduction and explicitly attempting to create noncapitalist social relations through an emphasis on political pedagogies.

The pandemic, even if only briefly, functioned as an opening for questions about the interdependence of all life and responsibilities for collective care and reproduction. It allowed for recognizing how we are affected by others and how our actions affect those to whom we are connected. It raised questions about what labor is truly essential and how that labor is (under)valued. The contradiction between capital and life became exceptionally clear, but, at the same time, desires for other ways of living were publicly acknowledged and debated. Struggles over reproduction took center stage and mutual aid networks and other grassroots responses to the multiple overlapping crises proliferated.

But we also saw our labor multiply during the pandemic, becoming trapped in the household with fewer opportunities to politicize and collectivize it. Mapping our labors, then, is not only to map our exploitation, but also to map where we have power, where we can refuse to labor, and the possibilities for collectivization. This is why the practical exercise of mapping through the feminist strike is so powerful: not as a representation, but as an intervention into the territory itself by removing women's and feminized labor from the territory, rendering it visible through its absence.

The question remains how we can expand the power of the feminist strike and harness the opening provided by the pandemic to continue asking questions about what it would mean to truly put collective life in the center of our political and economic decisions. How we can expand our map of connections, solidarities, and alliances not only across borders, but in ways that challenge those very borders and separations? How can we use this exercise to imagine, and to enact, other possible forms of our collective reproduction?

3. POSTSCRIPT ON THE EMERGENCY SOCIETY

I. LOGIC OF THE EMERGENCY

THE HOME AS *Laboratory* [*La casa como laboratorio*], originally published in Argentina in 2021, is an artifact-book that contains research, reflections, and resonances with movements produced during the COVID-19 pandemic. Two years after its publication, we can affirm that the economic and political dynamics it analyzes have only *intensified*. More than anything, we could say that they have imposed an *emergency continuum*. It is no longer a matter of a state of exception, but rather a constantly renewed emergency.

Over what spaces is this emergency continuum imposed? In our work, we have returned to feminist debates that have pointed to the importance of understanding the historically devalued domestic space, in order to render visible mutations in capital valorization. We do so from a conjuncture that has marked a "before and after" at the global level. What happened during the pandemic continues interrupting everyday life and reorganizing the world. It has intervened in subjectivation at the global scale. It is a mark whose symptoms are felt on mental health in a generalized way.

The novelty of the pandemic, we argued, has been experienced in relation to a series of issues—affective, political, and conceptual—that the feminist movement has brought to the forefront on a mass scale in recent years. Specifically, we are referring to how the question of labor exploitation and contemporary forms of the privatization of social reproduction have acquired marked importance in the heat of feminist mobilizations and strikes. But, we are also referring to changes in sexo-affective relations and the politicization of interdependence, not only among people but also with nonhumans and the land.

The political centrality acquired by the terrain of social reproduction, the re-emergence of this "idea-force," is not merely an academic debate and even less a technical one: it is an element of feminist struggles over these years. It is those struggles which have been able to make the most accurate diagnoses about contemporary capitalism's forms of exploitation, domination, and violence. Based on those diagnoses, they have challenged race, class, and gender privileges to think about and inhabit interdependence in other ways.

Analyzing the home as a laboratory, as we have proposed here, put the emphasis on the rentier aspect of capital: that which seems to be more abstract and, at the same time, expands into spaces where gender mandates are disputed, where precarity and the exploitation of unpaid labor are most brutally experienced today. Rent, as a formula of value, seems to increasingly require the emergency. Extractive dynamics accelerate over it. That extraction takes place over bodies and territories.

From that premise, we went back to thinking about homes as sites of new enclosures: spaces of financial recolonization for capital, where debts have continued accumulating due to the global increase in energy, food, and housing prices. The pandemic, we believe, has attempted a maneuver of reprivatization, a sort of "call to order" to the street occupation pushed by feminisms and their ways of subverting heteropatriarchal domesticity. In fact, the "factory-homes" activated in the pandemic (a term that we take from the 1970s, however today no longer surrounded by the correlate of Fordist factories) continue being subjected to extraordinary conditions, even after the COVID-19 emergency. This continuum is a neuralgic point of our current reflections. Today we believe that how we collectively process these transformations that are still underway will determine our capacity of political rearticulation, to sustain struggles, and revitalize agendas.

By speaking of factory-homes, we are not "skipping" the properly neoliberal enterprise-form. Nor are we taking a step backwards to return to the factory form. Rather, we are interested in understanding and problematizing how the overlap of certain factory forms is assembled for reproduction in connection with debtor mandates for those who are required to be entrepreneurs of the self and consumers of cheap platform services.

Gilles Deleuze animalized currency to think about the shift from disciplinary society to the society of control. He said, "The old monetary mole is the animal of the spaces of enclosure, but the serpent is that of the societies of control."[1] What can we say about virtual wallets, algorithmic credit, and debt as popular currency? What

---

1 Gilles Deleuze, "Postscript on the Societies of Control," *October*, Vol. 59 (Winter 1992): 3–7.

animal would be appropriate to characterize its way of moving?

Marketing is now considered old-fashioned. The company already supposes an overly fixed structure. The retreat is toward something that existed earlier and, at the same time, that is completely reorganized: the domestic assisted by platform tentacles, intermittent incomes, and a speculative cavalcade to survive precarity.

II. DISCIPLINE, CONTROL, AND PANDEMIC

THE COST OF social reproduction continues being offloaded onto these homes, understood as simultaneously microscopic and global spaces. Rate increases for basic services impoverish and alter the everyday lives of millions of people, demonstrating which spaces accumulate the "costs" of the current reconfiguration. At the same time, war is once again used as the discourse to internationally legitimize austerity policies toward certain nation-states.

The war in Ukraine, as a continuation by other means of several of the trends that intensified during the pandemic, exacerbated the phenomenon of inflation that was already foreshadowed at the beginning of the health emergency, with the disruption and cost increase of global commodity logistics. It shut down discussions that had been opened with great effort over what deserves public spending and what collective care look like, and strengthened militarized and securitized, racist and family-centered wagers.

In the case of Argentina, we are facing an extreme situation: inflation is over 100 percent annually and leads to very quick everyday impoverishment. Here, where we are writing from, we continue experiencing how the renegotiations with the international lending agencies that hold the foreign debt continue limiting the capacity for social spending and minimal redistributive measures.[2] At the same time, they propose the "financial inclusion" of populations who were already indebted due to the loss of income and accumulated inflation. Thus, a sort of "debt line" is drawn, evoking the "color line" of W. E. B. Du Bois' pioneering research on the United States. In the debt line we can see the colonial variable of financial capitalism and what Paula Chakravarty and Denise Ferreira da Silva call "the racial logic of global capitalism."[3]

It is no coincidence, then, that, after the pandemic, we see the increasing importance of movements defending the right to housing against financial speculation, demanding rental regulations, and taking concrete actions against evictions. Here we find another echo with the 2008 crisis. The feminist perspective on the housing crisis allows, once again, for understanding how movements of financialization touch down in everyday life, in specific terrains of dispute. Thus, it shows how ways of "insecuritizing" social reproduction are a key component of the rising conservative reaction.

As Rolnik, Andrade Guerreiro, and Marín-Toro emphasize, in Latin America, rent has become the new frontier that connects the financial sector with the real-estate sec-

---

2 In 2018, Mauricio Macri, president at the time, took out a 57 billion dollar loan. In 2021, the economic minister Martín Guzmán took out a new Extended Facilities loan to meet the unpayable deadlines of the prior agreement that implies quarterly reviews by IMF officials and particularly conditions social policies.

3 Paula Chakravarty and Denise Ferreira da Silva, "Accumulation, Dispossession and Debt: The Racial Logic of Global Capitalism," *American Quarterly* 64, no. 3: (2012): 361–385.

tor.[4] In this way, the flexibilization of rental relations are a component of the production of insecurity in the reproduction of life, at the same time as the management of that insecurity is proposed through temporary rentals that increase financial profits.

Airbnb types of platforms reorder neighborhoods and cities and the chances of accessing a rental. The inflationary crisis has de facto dollarized the price of rents to the point that the forms of its regulation establish a pitched battle with forms of financial speculation. Furthermore, the increase in rent functions as a *mechanism of direct extraction* over wages; in other words: more rent, less income. This seems key to us because rents are a fundamental dimension of generalized precarization and that of workers in particular. This also means that homes become "units of financial calculation," as Dick Bryan, Randy Martin, and Mike Rafferty have indicated.[5] Additionally, they emphasize how the reproduction of the labor force is increasingly tied to credit and depends on the value of the interest rate, which necessarily reconfigures our understanding of class relations.

Our organizations have been insisting that we need policies to guarantee housing access in opposition to real-estate speculation, because female heads of household, lesbians, gays, travesti, and trans people are the most affected by this concentrated and abusive market. When the real-estate

4 Raquel Rolnik, Isadora Andrade Guerreiro, and Andrea Marín-Toro, "El arriendo -formal e informal- como nueva frontera de la financiarización de la vivienda en América Latina," *Revista INVI* 36, no. 103 (2021): 19–53.

5 Dick Bryan, Randy Martin, and Mike Rafferty, "Financialization and Marx: Giving Labor and Capital a Financial Makeover," *Review of Radical Political Economics* 41, no. 4 (Fall 2009): 458–472.

market concentrates power, it means that it governs. It governs because it has the capacity to decide who lives in the city and who does not. In other words, it decides what lives deserve to inhabit a city that is advertised as being for everyone, yet is increasingly for fewer and fewer. Rental market regulations are profoundly feminist policies. The rental market, in turn, is inseparable from ever-increasing practices of land grabs.

Simultaneously, the population living on the streets or in hotels increases. So-called "family hotels"—that are not transitory nor for tourists as the name would suggest, but rather function as social holding blocks—charge by the night. A person can pay for a night in a hotel to shower, sleep, and later, back to the streets until, after a few weeks, they save up the money to get a roof over their head for at least one night. These situations operate for those who were already eliminated from the "scoring" and, according to the real-estate market, "do not qualify."

To "pull the rug out from under you" is a common expression for the experience of destablization. The metaphor, not without reason, is domestic. Not being able to guarantee housing exposes us to radical uncertainty. It connects us to panic-made-flesh because it is the very experience of lacking shelter in the world. Is it not this situation—both intimate and massive today—that is the source of a terrorized subjectivity? It is not this abysmal defenselessness that produces a sort of reaction in the face of politics that is governed by electoral calendars? It certainly does. At the same time, it poses a concrete challenge to our organizations and collective networks that wager on building community in opposition to the attempts to channel these fears in reactionary directions.

III. PROGRAM

ONE OF THE most important issues is the challenge that this situation poses to unions. We are convinced that the reinvention of the strike tool by the feminist movement at the transnational level since 2017 is a key element in the proliferation of strikes today, especially in sectors such as healthcare (nurses in particular) and platform workers (delivery workers in their varied modes). More generally, the feminist strike continues intervening in union dynamics that accompany and politicize the crisis of social reproduction. It is in this sense that we can glimpse a horizon of feminist unionism.

In this sequence of mobilization and organization, the debate has expanded over how these forms of historically devalued, feminized, and nonrecognized work are connected to waged labor, with the different inequalities that are expressed in the labor market, as well as the wage gap. This sexual and colonial division of labor establishes a hierarchy in the origins of the system that fundamentally structures social relations as a whole.

Analyses and forms of protest linked to the women, lesbians, travestis, trans peoples, migrants, and peasants' labor has taken a new impulse, becoming an issue for collective elaboration and public confrontation like never before. Particularly, these feminist perspectives and struggles have shown how these forms of exploitation and the economic violence that they involve are fundamentally and structurally connected with sexist violence. This way of conceptualizing and understanding labor in a feminist register is not only analytic. It has involved politically articulating demands, thinking about organization in collective terms, and instigating practical coordination experiments.

This problematization of labor by the feminist movement in its most recent international cycle can be woven and read based on a meshwork of slogans that have become emblematic, such as "if our lives don't matter, produce without us," "all women are workers," "we strike against the precarization of life." At the global level the organization of the feminist strike and, more generally, the intersection between feminists in movements and feminists in unions and their articulation with social and Indigenous movements has produced innovations in modes of organization, types of political alliances, and spaces of convergence and articulation. In this sense, diverse experiences have occurred that allow for exploring and reflecting on feminist unionism's new organizational forms, both in and outside of unions, and, more than anything, have allowed for expanded spaces of articulation.

These new organizational forms of feminist unionism have several dynamics, as they: 1) update long-standing union trajectories at the same time as they encourage new groupings—for example, creating spaces for women unionists and strengthening existing gender spaces within unions; 2) they invent new union-type strategies—for example, taking union dynamics to other struggles; 3) they produce mixed forms through contemporary labor and feminist conflicts that were previously invisibilized or not recognized as such—for example, regarding issues such as abortion, pension reform, or gender-based violence; 4) they reformulate organic instances of coordination, including new subjects and conflicts—for example, through inter-union organizations, coordinating bodies, assemblies in the midst of conflicts, and interventions in union and parliamentary debates; 5) they reconfigure union and feminist agendas, reinventing what "belongs" to each and what is in common between them.

Feminist unionism's organizational forms thus expand the field of struggles, call attention to unpaid labor, dispute and demand its recognition, at the same time as they demand resources that include and, at the same time, go beyond the wage. These forms of feminist unionism are a laboratory of political action for new worker subjectivities. They are also trial runs for materializing the demands that have been launched through the feminist strike against the precarization of life.

The strike, through feminism, is differentiated from the traditional labor strike (that is from the masculine, waged, and unionized labor movement), because it does not function as a tool that is only linked to classified and recognized jobs, tasks, and "professions." The feminist movement has made explicit how spaces of social reproduction are directly productive spaces. And, furthermore, it connects why production in capitalism is sustained by social reproduction, at the same time, as it hides that inevitable connection, where it locates the nucleus of the sexual and international division of labor. Social reproduction thus illuminates the decisive importance of housing, education, pensions, community and neighborhood work, forms of collective care, childcare, and everything that reproduces social life. But it also shows how those spaces, where all of that takes place, have been systematically attacked by structural adjustment plans, by privatization, by cuts to public budgets, and neoliberal commodification.

Therefore, feminist unionism, associated with the struggle over social reproduction, also demonstrates a common plane for struggles and demands that at first appear segmented and disperse. Following this path, the feminist movement has transformed how conflicts emerge in those spheres. The challenge of organizing other dynamics of making claims, demands, vindications, and negotiation is redrawn.

A debate inaugurated by feminists in the 1970s has been called up again: what would a wage for reproductive tasks look like? In turn, the politicization of reproduction work has had an impact on union agendas in the formal labor market, as well as in dynamics of the informalization of employment. Demands, for example, include equal leave for care work and social security systems that include the recognition of work carried out in the domestic sphere. Similarly, the politicization of social reproduction has implied going beyond the union agenda focused on wages, including struggles for access to housing and land and against financial exploitation. In moments of crisis sharpened by the pandemic, it became clear how urgent these issues were for explaining how economic, labor, and financial violences are interconnected with sexist violences. Feminist diagnoses have accounted for a multiplication of working days within the same day, the exhaustion involved in putting one's body on the line against the crisis, simultaneous tele-work with schooling in the home, constant juggling in the face of unemployment and reduced incomes, the replacement of the state's responsibilities with overburdened networks that never have enough resources.

Therefore, during the pandemic this debate has taken on a global dynamic that involves the majorities and is capable of using feminism's contributions to understand the crisis. For example, in the face of the growing quantity of unpaid work being carried out, we see the debate about a universal basic income appear in public debate. The feminist movement has taken a step further, also questioning the different ways in which monetary payouts imply forms of moralizing the lives of women, lesbians, travestis, and trans people, as well as all the associated entrepreneurial trappings.

An economy of fatigue, lack of time, and exhaustion accompanies the logic of emergency. This is assembled with the speculative theft of time practiced by finance in everyday life. The feminist strike also gives us clues about how to confront this: a reappropriation of time to make space for a political process capable of returning us to speculation over the future.

ABOUT THE AUTHORS

Luci Cavallero is coauthor of *A Feminist Reading of Debt*, with Verónica Gago. She has a PhD in Social Science, is a researcher at the Universidad de Buenos Aires, and member of the feminist collective Ni Una Menos (Not One More!). Her research focuses on debt and gender. She teaches in the Gender Studies Master's Program at the Universidad Nacional de Tres de Febrero. She is also the coauthor in Spanish of ¿Quién Le Debe *A Quién? Ensayos Transnacionales De Desobediencia Financiera*, with Silvia Federici and Verónica Gago (Tinta Limón-F. Rosa Luxemburgo, 2021).

Verónica Gago is the author of *Feminist International: How to Change Everything* and coauthor of *A Feminist Reading of Debt*, with Luci Cavallero. She is also part of the #NiUnaMenos movement (Not One More!), as both a theoretician and an activist. She is a Professor of Social Sciences at the University of Buenos Aires, Professor at the Instituto de Altos Estudios, Universidad Nacional de San Martín, and Independent Researcher at the National Council of Research (CONICET). Her work is deeply influenced by active participation in the experience of Colectivo Situaciones, whose *19 and 20* and *Genocide in the Neighborhood* recorded the Argentine social movements around the 2001 debt crisis with remarkable acuity.

LIZ MASON-DEESE HOLDS a PhD in Geography from the University of North Carolina at Chapel Hill. She is a member of the Counter-Cartographies Collective, the Viewpoint Magazine Editorial Collective, and the translation collective Territorio de Ideas. Among other works, she has translated *The Feminist Subversion of the Economy* by Amaia Pérez Orozco (Common Notions, 2022), *A Feminist Reading of Debt* by Luci Cavallero and Verónica Gago (Pluto Press, 2021), and *Feminist International: How to Change Everything* by Verónica Gago (Verso Books, 2020).

ABOUT COMMON NOTIONS

COMMON NOTIONS is a publishing house and programming platform that fosters new formulations of living autonomy. We aim to circulate timely reflections, clear critiques, and inspiring strategies that amplify movements for social justice.

Our publications trace a constellation of critical and visionary meditations on the organization of freedom. By any media necessary, we seek to nourish the imagination and generalize common notions about the creation of other worlds beyond state and capital. Inspired by various traditions of autonomism and liberation—in the US and internationally, historical and emerging from contemporary movements—our publications provide resources for a collective reading of struggles past, present, and to come.

Common Notions regularly collaborates with political collectives, militant authors, radical presses, and maverick designers around the world. Our political and aesthetic pursuits are dreamed and realized with Antumbra Designs.

www.commonnotions.org
info@commonnotions.org

MORE FROM
COMMON NOTIONS

Grupo de Arte Callejero: Thought, Practices, and Actions
Grupo de Arte Callejero

Translated by the Mareada Rosa Translation Collective

ISBN: 978-1-942173-10-6 (print)
ISBN: 978-1-942173-34-2 (eBook)
$22.00 | 6 x 9 | 352 pages
Subjects: Art/Latin America/Social Theory

An indispensable reflection on what was done and what remains to be done in the social fields of art and revolution.

Grupo de Arte Callejero: Thought, Practices, and Actions tells the profound story of social militancy and art in Argentina over the last two decades and propels it forward. For Grupo de Arte Callejero [Group of Street Artists], militancy and art blur together in the anonymous, collective, everyday spaces and rhythms of life. Thought, Practices, and Actions offers an indispensable reflection on what was done and what remains to be done in the social fields of art and revolution.

Every new utopian struggle that emerges must to some extent be organized on the knowledge of its precedents. From this perspective, Grupo de Arte Callejero situates their experience in a network of previous and subsequent practices that based more on popular knowledge than on great theories. Their work does not elaborate a dogma or a model to follow, but humbly expresses their interventions within Latin American autonomous politics as a form of concrete, tangible support so that knowledge can be generalized and politicized by a society in movement.

Without a doubt this will not be the most exhaustive book that can be written on the GAC, nor the most complete, nor the most acute and critical, but it is the one GAC wanted to write for themselves.

BECOME A COMMON NOTIONS MONTHLY SUSTAINER

These are decisive times ripe with challenges and possibility, heartache, and beautiful inspiration. More than ever, we need timely reflections, clear critiques, and inspiring strategies that can help movements for social justice grow and transform society.

Help us amplify those words, deeds, and dreams that our liberation movements, and our worlds, so urgently need.

Movements are sustained by people like you, whose fugitive words, deeds, and dreams bend against the world of domination and exploitation.

For collective imagination, dedicated practices of love and study, and organized acts of freedom.
By any media necessary.
With your love and support.

Monthly sustainers start at $15.

commonnotions.org/sustain

MORE FROM
COMMON NOTIONS

*Genocide in the Neighborhood:
State Violence, Popular Justice, and the
'Escrache'*
Colectivo Situaciones
Translated by Brian Whitener

ISBN: 978-1-942173-86-1 (print)
ISBN: 978-1-945335-02-0 (eBook)
$20.00 | 6 x 9 | 128 pages
Subjects: Latin America/Insurrections/
Resistance

**Documents the theories, debates,
successes, and failures of a rebellious
tactic to build popular power.**

Genocide in the Neighborhood docu-
ments the autonomist practice of the "escrache," a system of public
shaming that emerged in the late 1990s to vindicate the lives of those dis-
appeared under the Argentinean dictatorship and to protest the amnesty
granted to perpetrators of the killing.

Through a series of hypotheses and two sets of interviews, *Genocide in the
Neighborhood* documents the theories, debates, successes, and failures of
the escraches—what Whitener defines as "something between a march,
an action or happening, and a public shaming—investigates the nature
of rebellion, discusses the value of historical and cultural memory to resistance, and suggests decentralized ways to agitate for justice.

The book follows the popular Argentine uprising in 2001, a period of
intense social unrest and political creativity that led to the collapse of government after government. The power that ordinary people developed for
themselves in public space soon gave birth to a movement of neighborhoods organizing themselves into hundreds of popular assemblies across
the country, the unemployed workers struggle mobilizing, and workers
taking over factories and businesses. These events marked a sea change,
a before and an after for Argentina that has since resonated around the
world. In its wake *Genocide in the Neighborhood* tactfully deploys a much
needed model of political resistance.

MORE FROM
COMMON NOTIONS

19 and 20: Notes for a New Insurrection
Colectivo Situaciones

With Contributions by Marcello Tarì,
Liz Mason-Deese, Antonio Negri, and
Michael Hardt
Translated by Nate Holdren and
Sebastian Touza

ISBN: 978-1-942173-48-9 (print)
ISBN: 978-1-942173-62-5 (eBook)
$20.00 | 6 x 9 | 288 pages
Subjects: Latin America/Insurrections/
Resistance

**From a rebellion against neoliberal-
ism's miserable failures, notes for a
new insurrection and a new society.**

19 and 20 tells the story of one of the most popular uprisings against neoliberalism: on December 19th and 20th, 2001, amidst a financial crisis
that tanked the economy, ordinary people in Argentina took to the streets
shouting "*¡Qué se vayan todos!*" (They all must go!) Thousands of people
went to their windows banging pots and pans, neighbors organized themselves into hundreds of popular assemblies, workers took over streets and
factories. In those exhilarating days, government after government fell as
people invented a new economy and a new way of governing themselves.

It was a defining moment of the antiglobalization movement and
Colectivo Situaciones was there, thinking and engaging in the struggle.
Their writings during the insurrection have since been passed hand to
hand and their practice of militant research modelled widely as a way of
thinking together in a time of rebellion. Today, as a staggering debt crisis
deepens, we see the embers from that time twenty years ago in the mutual
aid initiatives and new forms of solidarity amidst widespread vulnerability. Revisiting the forms of counterpower that emerged from the shadow
of neoliberal rule, Colectivo Situaciones reminds us that our potential is
collective and ungovernable.